CHINA'S ALLOCATION OF FIXED CAPITAL INVESTMENT, 1952-1957

Chu-yuan Cheng

MICHIGAN PAPERS IN CHINESE STUDIES
No. 17   1974

THE UNIVERSITY OF MICHIGAN
CENTER FOR CHINESE STUDIES

MICHIGAN PAPERS IN CHINESE STUDIES
NO. 17

CHINA'S ALLOCATION OF FIXED
CAPITAL INVESTMENT, 1952-1957

By
Chu-yuan Cheng
Professor of Economics
Ball State University, Indiana

Ann Arbor

Center for Chinese Studies
The University of Michigan

1974

ACKNOWLEDGMENTS

Much of the basic research and writing of this monograph was completed while I was a Senior Research Economist at the Center for Chinese Studies at The University of Michigan. As is generally the case, this paper could not have appeared in its present form without the aid of many friends and colleagues. Particularly, I must single out the unstinting efforts of Professor Albert Feuerwerker in providing the inspiration as well as arranging the myriad of details necessary for publication. I would be immodest indeed if I failed to mention my indebtedness to Professor Alexander Eckstein whose critical acumen saved the author from many a pitfall. Errors of omission and commission, however, are solely my responsibility.

I would also like to thank my colleagues at Ball State University who provided me with the constant encouragement and a lightened teaching load that enabled me to revise and update my initial work.

C. Y. Cheng
Muncie, Indiana
June 1974

TABLE OF CONTENTS

iii

iv

LIST OF STATISTICAL TABLES

vii

Chapter I

INTRODUCTION

The significance of capital formation for economic growth has been widely discussed in the economic literature over the past two decades. Its importance has now become almost a self-evident fact requiring no further elaboration. In recent years, the study of capital formation in Mainland China has attracted growing attention from scholars in the field of Chinese economy. Most of the available studies, however are concerned primarily with problems relating to the measurement of the aggregate levels of capital formation, the overall rates of investment and the relationships between capital formation and the changing rates of economic growth. The allocation of investment among different economic sectors, and among various branches within each sector, has been only touched peripherally without delving in detail. The purpose of the paper is to fill this gap. It aims at studying primarily the allocation of fixed capital formation in Mainland China.

In an early study comparing capital formation in the Soviet Union and in the United States, Norman Kaplan observed that the Soviet Union's greater rate of increase in industrial output and economic growth has been due, basically, not to the differences in USSR and United States rates of investment,[1] but rather to the differences in the allocation of that investment. In the periods for which his comparison was made, the USSR and the U.S. rates of investment in non-war years were roughly equal. However, the share of industry in total Soviet investment has far exceeded the corresponding United States ratios (35-40 percent in USSR against 20-25 percent in the US). Meanwhile, the Soviet share of investment in the metal products industries as compared to total investment was more than 1.5 times that in the United States.[2]

Similar conclusions were derived by Simon Kuznets in his extensive study of capital formation covering a wide range of countries. Kuznets noted that the distinctive intersectoral allocation of capital formation in the Communist countries has a significant bearing on their growth rates.[3]

Against this background, we would like to explore what role

did the intersectoral pattern of investment lay in Mainland China's economic growth. For this purpose, we need detailed information on the distribution of capital investment not only among the various economic sectors, but also among various branches within sectors. Such a study requires a large amount of disaggregated data. Because of the extreme paucity of relevant data, we are forced to limit our study to domestic fixed capital investment.

By domestic fixed capital investment we mean the additions to (1) construction and improvements attached to the land, and (2) producers' durable equipment. We exclude inventories and net balance of claims upon other countries. The concept of capital formation thus defined is narrow indeed. Moreover, the study also excludes consumer durables (except housing), and military equipment and installations.

This study covers only the 1952-57 period, when statistical data were comparatively abundant and the rapid growth rates which require explanation were experienced. Years before 1952 are not included because of the poor quality of the data and because this is mainly a recovery rather than a development period. For the post-1958 period information is particularly scarce. Therefore a detailed analysis becomes infeasible.

While the focus of this paper is on the allocation pattern of investment, it must first of all, select one set of aggregate investment estimates to work with. Unfortunately, the official data on basic construction investment is conceptually different from the standard concepts of fixed capital investment. Also, there are many fundamental defects in the official statistics of investment aggregates which are difficult to correct. Among the half dozen estimates of aggregate capital formation for China by scholars outside the mainland, there is not yet one commonly accepted. A major study of this problem was undertaken by K. C. Yeh.[4] Yeh's estimate is based on Chinese official investment data with adjustments made for conceptual differences and statistical undercoverage so as to render it more comparable to Western concepts. Since his estimate is not independently constructed, it cannot be completely free from the defects of official data. More recently Kang Chao derived a series of aggregate investment by using the commodity flow method.[5] Chao's estimates represent the first major effort to derive an independent estimate bypassing the official investment data.

Despite his ingenious innovations in solving many data problems, Chao's estimates suffer from two basic biases. First, since major repairs of machinery and machines turned out by handicrafts were excluded, the machinery component of the estimate is understated. Second, since a sizable private investment in rural housing was imputed and which was possibly overestimated, the investment share between farm and non-farm sectors is grossly distorted.

Confronting these problems, we begin our study with a brief survey of official investment statistics and those made by economists outside mainland China. A detailed review is devoted to Chao's estimates, which are used as a basis for this study. Necessary adjustments are made to eliminate the biases embodied in Chao's aggregates.

Based on the adjusted aggregates, the study will turn to the allocation pattern of investment. The aggregate investment in fixed capital will be first broken down into five major economic sectors: agriculture, industry, transportation and communications, residential construction and other services. An attempt is then made to measure the sectoral average and incremental capital-output ratios, as a basis for analyzing Chinese investment policy. Fixed investments in the industrial sector are then again disaggregated into thirteen industrial branches: iron and steel, building materials, chemical, non-ferrous metals, machine-building, metal-processing, coal, textiles, electricity, petroleum, food-processing, paper-making and others. This will be followed by an effort to distribute the aggregate investment in the agricultural sector into six major components: water conservation, livestock, farm implements, afforestation, land reclamation, and others.

Our analysis concludes with an overall assessment of the distinctive features of the Chinese investment allocation pattern at both the sectoral and branch level, its possible effect on industrial development and economic growth, as well as its significance for other developing countries. Tentative as they are, it is hoped that the findings can bring to light some hitherto neglected elements that contribute to China's economic growth.

4

FOOTNOTES

1. Norman M. Kaplan, "Capital Formation and Allocation," in Abram Bergson (ed), <u>Soviet Economic Growth, Conditions and Perspective,</u> (Evanston, Illinois, Row, Peterson, 1953), p. 80.

2. <u>Ibid.</u>, p. 65.

3. Simon Kuznets, "Capital Formation Proportions," in <u>Economic Development and Cultural Change,</u> Vol. 8, No. 4, Part II (July 1960), p. 43.

4. K. C. Yeh, "Capital Formation in Mainland China, 1931-36, and 1952-57," (Unpublished dissertation, Columbia University), 1965.

5. Kang Chao, "Fixed Capital Investment in Communist China" (unpublished manuscript), 1968. Chao's work will be published by the California University Press. The data quoted in this paper are from the 1968 manuscript.

Chapter II

ESTIMATES OF TOTAL FIXED CAPITAL INVESTMENT

Statistical data on "basic construction investment" and "new fixed assets," two concepts close to fixed capital investment, are available in Chinese official sources covering the period 1952-57. During the past decade, there have also been about half a dozen estimates of China's capital formation derived by economists outside China. Since most of these estimates are constructed on the basis of official data with various adjustments, it seems appropriate to begin this chapter with a brief review of the official statistics. We will then discuss estimates made by two Western scholars and derive our own adjusted figures for fixed capital investment.

(1) Official Investment Statistics

For the First Five-Year Plan period (1953-57), information about "accumulation" and "capital stock" is fairly abundant, in scattered official sources. The quality of capital investment statistics has been ranked by a Communist authority as better than statistics on agricultural output and trade but inferior to those on industrial production.[1] The defects of Chinese statistics and the pitfalls in using them have been examined by other economists in the United States and in Japan, and it is not necessary to repeat them here.[2] It is sufficient to say that Chinese official statistics for capital investment have a number of complications and require close scrutiny. Also, they have no exact equivalent in China to what we have defined in the United States as fixed capital formation.

The term "accumulation" as used in official literature comes fairly close to the Western concept of net domestic investment. It is defined as "the sum of the increase in productive and non-productive fixed assets and the increase in working capital and stockpiles."[3] Since the term excludes both depreciation and claims against foreign countries, it can be regarded as equivalent to net domestic investment.

The widely used term "basic construction investment" is quite similar to the Western concept of fixed capital formation. Essentially it refers to the purchase costs of tools and equipment plus the value of construction activities. There are two basic

5

differences between the Chinese concept of basic construction investment and the Western concept of fixed capital investment: the
Chinese concept (a) excludes major repairs, which are considered
part of fixed capital formation in the West, and (b) includes some
ancillary expenses, such as costs of training personnel to operate
the new projects and compensation for the loss of property, which
are not considered as investment in Western practice. [4]

The term "new fixed assets" used in Chinese statistics
resembles gross investment in physical capital. However, its
coverage is more limited, and the definition changes. Before 1956,
"fixed assets" were articles worth more than 500 yuan with a life
span of more than one year. Those below these criteria were
classified as "low value or perishable articles." In 1956 the minimum
value for "fixed assets" was lowered to only 200 yuan.

Confusing as they are, however, the differences in terminology
are not the main reason rejecting the official statistics. Once the
definitions are clarified, proper adjustments can be made to render
the categories comparable to Western usage. Kang Chao has pointed
out that the fundamental defects of the official data given in Table 1
rest on two other grounds: the changing coverage of some categories
of investment magnitude and the use of unreasonable bases for
valuation. An example of the first defect is the change in definition
of fixed assets from 500 yuan to 200 yuan, which renders the figures
on "fixed assets" before and after 1956 incomparable. Examples of
the second defect are the underestimation of the costs of construction
projects done by forced labor and the application of divergent rates
of foreign exchange in valuing machinery and equipment imported
from the Soviet bloc and non-Communist countries. Since most of
these problems are difficult to correct, an independent estimate based
on less aggregate data is indispensable for studying capital formation
in China.

(2) Estimates by Yeh and Chao

In the late 1950s and early 1960s several attempts were made
to construct estimates of Chinese capital formation. The best known
are those by William Hollister, Alexander Eckstein, C. M. Li, and
S. Ishikawa. [5] However, capital formation was only part of their
broader analyses, and they did not focus on this particular topic. [6]

The first study devoted exclusively to this subject was done
by K. C. Yeh. Yeh's pre-war estimates, derived by the commodity

Table 1

OFFICIAL DATA ON INVESTMENT, 1952–57
(IN MILLION YUAN)

	1952	1953	1954	1955	1956	1957
Accumulation, at current prices	11,440	16,071	17,333	17,390	20,905	19,839
Accumulation, at 1952 prices	11,440	16,037	17,375	18,177	23,010	22,171
Basic construction, within the state plan, at current prices	3,710	6,510	7,500	8,630	13,990	12,640
Basic construction, outside the state plan, at current prices	650	1,490	1,570	670	810	1,190
Total basic construction at current prices	4,360	8,000	9,070	9,300	14,800	13,830
New fixed assets, at current prices	3,110	6,560	7,370	8,020	11,160	12,920

Source: Compiled by Nai-Ruenn Chen, Chinese Economic Statistics, A Handbook for Mainland China (Chicago: Aldine, 1967), pp. 141–145, 158, and 163.

flow method, made a significant breakthrough in this complicated subject. His estimates for the 1952-57 period, however, were still
based on official investment data, with adjustments to make them
comparable to Western concepts. Yeh's adjustments to the official
figures included (1) the deduction of non-investment elements (such
as ancillary expenses and costs of purchasing existing assets,
etc.), (2) the addition of major repairs, (3) the addition of values
for using work brigades and prisoners, (4) the addition of private
investments in urban and rural areas, and (5) the deduction of
overestimates for hog increases in 1956-57. [7]

Since Yeh's estimates were an adjustment of official statistics,
certain defects of the official statistics were inevitably retained.
Moreover, his breakdown of aggregate investment into construction
and equipment was derived by two steps: first the magnitude
of construction output was derived from official data on national
income by industrial origin; second, construction value was deducted
from total fixed investment to obtain the value for equipment. Since
equipment was treated as a residual any error in the estimation of
the construction would automatically affect the figure for equipment.

In attempting to construct an estimate that was independent of
official investment statistics, Kang Chao used the commodity flow
method to derive a series for aggregate fixed investment. His
estimates for the First Five-Year Plan period consisted of the
following component series: (1) construction and installations, (2) domestic production of machinery and equipment, (3) net imports of
machinery and equipment, (4) office furniture and tools, and (5) other
rural investments.

Chao's estimates are compared with official data and Yeh's and
others' estimates in Table 2. The comparison shows that both
Chao's and Yeh's estimates are uniformly higher than the official
data for basic construction investment. The discrepancies between
the official data and these two external estimates are due to the
narrower coverage of the official data. Since the portion omitted
from the official data (mainly private investment in rural areas) had
a relatively slow growth rate, the over-all rate of increase shown in
the official data is higher than that shown in the other two estimates.

There are also substantial differences between Chao's and
Yeh's estimates. For all the years, Chao's estimates are higher
than Yeh's; the difference ranges from 1.27 billion yuan in 1952 to

Table 2

COMPARISON OF VARIOUS ESTIMATES OF FIXED INVESTMENT, 1952-57 (MILLION YUAN)

	Chao's estimates of gross fixed investment (at constant 1952 prices)	Official data for basic construction investment (at current prices)	Liu-Yeh's gross fixed investment estimate I (at constant 1952 prices)	Liu-Yeh's gross fixed investment, estimate II	Yeh's gross fixed investment (at current prices)	Hollister's gross fixed investment (at current prices)	Ishikawa's net fixed investment (at current prices)
	(1)	(2)	(3)	(4)	(5)	(6)	(7)
1952	8,002	4,360	7,440	7,610	6,730	8,420	–
1953	11,378	8,000	11,250	11,880	9,790	12,590	10,029
1954	13,688	9,070	12,860	13,070	11,250	14,120	11,853
1955	15,207	9,300	14,070	15,510	12,500	13,920	12,671
1956	22,251	14,800	19,270	23,500	20,150	19,870	19,812
1957	20,541	13,830	21,610	22,160	18,880	18,770	17,950
Index for 1957 (1952=100)	256.7	317.0	290.5	291.2	280.5	222.9	

Table 2 (cont'd)

Sources: Column (1): Chao, op. cit., Table 7.
Column (2): Ten Great Years: Statistics of the Economic and Cultural Achievements of the People's Republic of China (Peking: State Statistical Bureau, 1960), p. 55.

Column (3): Ta-Chung Liu and Kung-Chia Yeh The Economy of the Chinese Mainland, National Income and Economic Development, 1933-59 (Princeton University Press, 1965), p. 74.

Column (4): Ibid., pp. 706, 74.
Column (5): Chao, op. cit., Table 8.
Column (6): W. W. Hollister, "Trends in Capital Formation in Communist China," in U.S. Congress Joint Economic Committee, An Economic Profile of Mainland China (1967), p. 151.

Column (7): Ishikawa, op. cit., pp. 145, 188.

2.7 billion yuan in 1955. Since the total divergence amounts to 30 percent, it cannot be attributed to any minor cause. According to Chao, 97.5 percent of the discrepancy of 12,307 million yuan over the 1952-57 period comes from their difference in rural housing investment. Without this difference, the two estimates would be very close, even though they were derived by two entirely different methods.

Yeh's figures for rural housing investment were based on a 1957 official survey of 228 typical agricultural producers' coopera- [8] tives selected from 24 provinces and regions throughout the country. From the results of this survey, Yeh estimated that rural housing construction in 1957 amounted to 230 million yuan. The 1957 figure was then multiplied by a gross value-added index for agricultural output to derive rural housing investment for the years 1952-56. Yeh materially underestimated rural housing investment because he misinterpreted the survey data. The survey evidently covered only housing owned by the agricultural cooperatives collectively and did not include housing owned by individual peasant households. Since Yeh took the survey data to cover both cooperatives and individuals, he in fact underestimated rural housing investment by a large margin.

Chao, on the other hand, overcorrected Yeh's estimate by imputing a huge investment in rural construction. The rationale and procedure Chao used to derive his rural housing investment figures can be summarized as follows:

(1)   Two sets of official data on the total output value of the building industry were used; one covered construction both within and outside the state plan, and the other covered only construction within the state plan. Chao reasoned that the difference between these two sets of data represented private construction. [9]

(2)   He then estimated that 90 percent of the private building investment was rural housing investment since all major construction in the urban areas must have been included in the state plan.

Using these assumptions, Chao assigned 90 percent of the difference between these two sets of official data as the annual investment in rural housing. On examination, however, these assumptions are difficult to sustain, or at least questionable.

In the first place, the difference between these two sets of official data is not completely due to the inclusion or exclusion of private construction works; it is also partly due to the inclusion or exclusion of "major repairs." According to Chao's own account, the first set of official data is "gross of depreciation and includes all repair works."[10] It includes all "replacements of old houses and structures and all repair works."[11] The second set of data, according to Chao, "does not include repair works."[12] In other words, the second set of data covers only the output value of state activities in building and installation, without including repairs.[13] Since it does not take into account the differences in major repairs, Chao's assignment of all the discrepancy to private investment in construction inevitably imparts an excess at least equal to the value of major repairs in the construction sector.

Secondly, Chao's decision to assign 90 percent of private construction to rural housing is also disputable. Until 1955, the private sector still constituted an important part of the urban economy. Between 1952 and 1955 the industrial fixed assets owned by private and joint public-private industry increased by 872 million yuan.[14] If 70 percent of these fixed assets consisted of construction, total private construction in these three years amounted to 610 million yuan, representing an average annual investment of more than 200 million yuan. This amount alone exceeds the 10 percent allowance made by Chao for these years. If we add construction investments by private commerce, cooperatives, handicrafts, and residential housing, the figure might well reach 20 percent of the total private construction investment.[15]

In addition, Chao's estimates for domestic production of machinery and equipment did not include major repairs in producer durables (which accounted for 30 percent of machine-building output in 1952). Since Chao's construction output did include major repairs, the omission of major repairs in the value of equipment creates an inconsistency in the coverages of these two components.[16]

Moreover, Chao's machinery output series covered only the output of modern factories and handicraft workshops, excluding the output of individual handicraftsmen and handicraft cooperatives. In the rural areas, the handicraft industries produce many capital goods, such as oil pressing machines, stone mills, wooden boats, fish nets, etc. According to one official statement, about one-fourth of the handicraftsmen were engaged in the production of producer goods.[17]

If half of the producer goods are durables, their omission would also introduce a downward bias into the value of producer durables.

As a result of these problems, Chao's estimates showed an exceptionally high proportion of construction in relation to equipment (Table 3).

According to Chao's estimates China's construction share far exceeded that in other underdeveloped countries, while the share of producer durables was below that in any other low-income country. In Kuznets' study of a number of countries, the share of construction in gross fixed capital formation varied from 59 percent in high-income countries to 61 percent in low-income countries. The share of producers' equipment varied correspondingly, from 41 to 39 percent. [18] Chao's estimate of 24.9 percent for producer durables is thus 40 percent lower than Kuznets' figures for other low-income countries.

This low share for producer durables also contradicts the Chinese Communist policy in price formation. According to the Liu-Yeh study, the price of construction in 1952 was estimated at three times that in 1933, while the price of equipment in 1952 was estimated at five times that in 1933. [19] This means that the 1952 price base gives a relatively large weight to investment in equipment. The low share of equipment estimated by Chao would imply a much lower share if the 1933 prices were used. This would put the share of producer durables in China even farther below that in other low-income countries.

Despite the defects mentioned above, however, Chao's estimates are used in this study, for two reasons. First, their biases are identifiable and can be corrected without great difficulty. Second, Chao's aggregates are derived by combining five separate series; the detailed information given in these component series is of great value for our study of the allocation of fixed investment.

(3) A Revised Estimate of Fixed Capital Investment

As we noted in the previous section, Chao overestimated rural housing investment because he failed to take into account major repairs in construction and he assigned only 10 percent allowance for private construction to the urban sector. In order to correct these upward biases, the first step is to estimate the magnitude of major repairs in the construction industry.

14

Table 3

DISTRIBUTION OF FIXED CAPITAL INVESTMENT
BETWEEN CONSTRUCTION AND PRODUCER DURABLES, 1952-57 (IN %)

	Official data[1]		Chao's estimate[2]		Yeh's estimate[3]	
	Construction	Producer Durables	Construction	Producer Durables	Construction	Producer Durables
1952	74.7	25.3	72.4	27.6	67.7	32.3
1953	74.5	25.5	73.6	26.4	67.9	32.1
1954	72.8	27.2	76.1	23.9	68.6	31.4
1955	66.3	33.7	74.8	25.2	64.7	35.3
1956	70.0	30.0	75.6	24.4	63.5	36.5
1957	70.0	30.0	76.0	24.0	62.4	37.6
1952-57	71.4	28.6	75.1	24.9	65.0	35.0

Sources: 1. Chu-Yuan Cheng, The Machine-Building Industry in Communist China, (Chicago: Aldine-Atherton 1971, pp. 43-44.
2. Chao, op. cit., p. 108.
3. Yeh, "Capital Formation," in Eckstein, Galenson, and Liu (eds.), Economic Trends in Communist China (Chicago: Aldine, 1968), p. 519.

There are no official data on major repairs in the total output value of the construction industry. The only information available is the total expense of major repairs for the entire public sector. In the First Five-Year Plan, a total of 3,600 million yuan was appropriated for major repairs.[20] In the same plan, the five-year total for capital construction investment was set at 4,274 million yuan, and the actual results were estimated at 115.3 percent of the original plan. Assuming the same performance ratio for major repairs, Ishikawa estimated the actual expenditure on major repairs for the period at 4,200 million yuan. If we allocate this total to each year in proportion to the annual values of fixed assets in the public sector and further assume that 70 percent of the fixed capital investment was for construction,[21] the annual values of major repairs for the construction industry can be estimated (Table 4).

Table 4

ESTIMATES OF MAJOR REPAIRS IN CONSTRUCTION AND
MACHINERY 1952-57 (IN MILLION YUAN)

	Total Major Repairs	Major Repairs for Construction[3]	Major Repairs for Machinery[4]
1952	400[1]	280	120
1953	570[2]	400	170
1954	700[2]	490	210
1955	910[2]	640	270
1956	940[2]	660	280
1957	1,120[2]	780	340
1952-57	4,640	3,250	1,390

Sources and notes:

1. K. C. Yeh, "Capital Formation," op. cit., p. 141.
2. Ishikawa, op. cit., p. 145.
3. Assumed to be 70% of total. (see footnote 21)
4. Residual.

The next problem is to assign a proper distribution between urban and rural private construction. As we have noted, for the 1952-55 period official data show that construction investment by private and joint public-private industries accounted for about 14 percent of the estimated total for private construction investment. [22] The addition of investments made for private commerce, handicrafts, and private housing would bring the share of urban private construction to at least 20 percent of the total. [23] The value of rural private housing investment derived under this assumption is given in Table 5.

The second item requiring adjustment is the addition of major repairs to the machinery component. The annual amounts are derived as shown in Table 4.

The final adjustment to be made is the addition of machinery and equipment turned out by handicraft cooperatives and individual handicraftsmen. Official data for this category are scanty. Between 1952 and 1957 the proportion of handicrafts in total industrial gross output value (including modern industry, handicraft workshops, and handicrafts) declined from 21.3 to 17.1 percent. In 1954, of the gross value of individual handicraft production, 22.96 percent was producer goods, [24] and 12.45 percent was industrial producer goods. The same official source also revealed that of the gross value of total handicraft production 6.03 percent was from metal manufacturing. Assuming that half of the metal-processing output by handicrafts was for producer durables, [25] the value of producer durables turned out by handicrafts can be estimated (Table 6).

Multiplying the percentages in the last column of Table 6 by the machinery output figures adjusted by Chao, the value of machinery turned out by handicrafts can be computed (Table 7).

The addition of major repairs and handicraft production to modern machinery output lifts the total machinery figure by 15 percent. The revised estimates of gross fixed capital formation during 1952-57 are summarized in Table 8.

Table 5

DERIVED VALUE OF RURAL HOUSING INVESTMENT, 1952-57 (IN MILLION YUAN)

	1952	1953	1954	1955	1956	1957
(1) Total output value of building industry (within and outside state plan)[1]	4,550	7,090	8,500	9,100	14,540	12,590
(2) Output value of building and installations (within state plan)[1]	2,800	5,660	6,460	6,690	10,560	9,560
(3) Difference between line 1 and line 2	1,750	1,430	2,040	2,410	3,980	2,940
(4) Major repairs in building industry[2]	280	400	490	640	660	780
(5) Private construction investment (line 3 minus line 4)	1,470	1,030	1,550	1,770	3,320	2,160
(6) Urban private construction[3] (20% of line 5)	290	210	310	350	660	450
(7) Rural private construction (line 5 minus line 6)	1,180	820	1,240	1,420	2,660	1,710

Sources: 1. Ishikawa, op. cit., p.72.
2. Table 4.
3. Assumed to be 20% of private construction; see footnote 23.

Table 6

PROPORTION OF MACHINERY TURNED OUT BY INDIVIDUAL HANDICRAFTSMEN, 1952-57

	1952	1953	1954	1955	1956	1957
(1) Output value of handicraft workshops and modern industry (million yuan)[1]	27,000	35,600	41,500	44,800	58,700	65,000
(2) Output value of individual handicraftsmen (million yuan)[2]	7,300	9,100	10,500	10,100	11,700	13,400
(3) Individual handicrafts as percent of line (1)[3]	27.0%	25.6%	25.3%	22.6%	20.0%	20.6%
(4) Machinery production as % of individual handicraft output[4]	3%	3%	3%	3%	3%	3%
(5) Individual handicraft machinery output as % of line (1)[5]	0.81%	0.77%	0.76%	0.68%	0.60%	0.62%
(6) Modern machinery output as % of line (1)[6]	5.2%	6.1%	6.4%	6.8%	9.8%	9.5%
(7) Individual handicraft machinery output as % of modern machinery output (5) ÷ (6)[7]	15.5%	12.6%	12.0%	10.0%	6.0%	6.5%

Sources and notes: 1. For 1952-55, Chinese Academy of Sciences, Economic Research Section, Handicraft Group, Editor, 1954-nien Ch'uan-kuo Ko-t'i Shou-kung-yeh Tiao-ch'a Tzu-liao.

Table 6

Sources and notes (continued):

      (Data of the 1954 Nation-wide Handicraft Investigation, Peking: San-lien-su-tien, 1957), p. 252. For 1956-57, Ten Great Years, p. 16.

2, Ten Great Years, p. 16
3. Row 2 divided by row 1.
4. According to the 1954 nation-wide handicraft investigation, in the gross value of total handicraft production of 13 important trades, metal manufacture accounted for 6.03 percent [Chao I-wen, Hsin-chung-kuo ti Kung-yeh (Peking: T'ung-chi Chu-pan-she, (1957), p. 103]. Here, I assume half of the metal manufacture was machine product similar to the proportion of machine output to modern industrial output value in the same year which was 49.7 percent.
5. Row 4 divided by row 1.
6. Chu-Yuan Cheng, The Machine-building industry in Communist China (Chicago: Aldine, 1971) Table 1, Chapter 2.
7. Row 5 divided by row 6.

Table 7

REVISED DOMESTIC MACHINERY OUTPUT, '
1952-57 (IN MILLION YUAN)

	(1) Machinery produced by modern industry	(2) Machinery turned out by handicrafts	(3) Major Repairs	(4) Total Domestic Machinery Output
1952	803	124	120	1,047
1953	1,072	135	170	1,377
1954	1,410	169	210	1,789
1955	1,862	186	270	2,318
1956	2,915	175	280	3,370
1957	2,471	161	340	2,972

Sources: column 1. Chao, op. cit., p. 50.
          column 2. Column (1) multiplied by line 7
                     of Table 6.
          column 3. Table 4.

The adjustments did not significantly affect the rate of growth of total gross fixed capital investment. Our 1957 index number is 255, compared with 256.7 as calculated by Chao. However, the adjustments did alter the structure of fixed capital investment during the First Plan period.

First, our adjusted estimates show a higher ratio of producer durables in the total gross fixed capital investment (Table 9). The average ratio for 1952-57 as calculated by Chao was 24.9 percent. Our adjusted ratio of 27 percent comes closer to the official data, which give 28.6 percent for this period.

Second, the adjusted estimates display a higher share of non-farm investment than do Chao's estimates. The non-farm proportion was 67.4 percent, compared with Chao's figure of 61 percent (Table 10)

Table 8

REVISED ESTIMATES OF GROSS FIXED CAPITAL INVESTMENT, 1952-57 (MILLION YUAN)

Year	(1) Construction and installations	(2) Domestic production of machinery and equipment	(3) Net imports of machinery and equipment	(4) Office furniture and tools	(5) Others	(6) Total	(7) Index
1952	4,789	1,047	524	47	1,846	8,253	100.0
1953	7,385	1,377	733	63	2,134	11,692	141.7
1954	9,401	1,789	700	75	2,144	14,079	170.6
1955	10,062	2,318	746	92	2,459	15,677	190.0
1956	15,622	3,370	1,148	136	2,714	22,990	278.6
1957	13,989	2,972	1,189	125	2,782	21,057	255.1

Sources: column 1: Chao, op. cit., p. 43.
         column 2: Table 7.
         column 3: Chao, Table 3, p. 69.
         column 4: Calculated at 3% of columns 2 and 3.
         column 5: Chao, Table 5, p. 80; this includes reclamation, old-
                   type implements, carts, and livestock, as well as
                   imputed investment.

Table 9

ADJUSTED DISTRIBUTION OF GROSS FIXED
CAPITAL INVESTMENT BETWEEN
CONSTRUCTION AND PRODUCER DURABLES, 1952-57

	Construction		Producer durables	
	Value (million yuan)	Share (%)	Value (million yuan)	Share (%)
1952	5,793	70.2	2,460	29.8
1953	8,373	71.5	3,319	28.5
1954	10,417	74.0	3,662	26.0
1955	11,382	73.6	4,295	27.4
1956	17,019	74.0	5,971	26.0
1957	15,610	74.0	5,447	26.0
1952-57	68,594	73.0	25,154	27.0

Note: Construction includes construction and installations and reclamation; producer durables include
domestic production of machinery and equipment,
net imports of machinery and equipment, office
furniture and tools and old-type implements,
carts and livestock.
Source: Table 8

Finally, the revised estimates of rural housing investment
(Table 11) are 5.8 times higher than Yeh's but 30 percent lower
than Chao's estimates. On a per capita basis, Chao's estimates
amount to 4.15 yuan annually for rural housing construction, while
Yeh gives only 0.46 yuan per annum. Our estimates result in
2.8 yuan per capita annually, which is more in accordance with the
real rural situation in China. An official sample survey of economic
conditions for 600 peasant households in five agricultural cooperatives
revealed that for each person in the household only 6.6 yuan in
1955 and 5.4 yuan in 1956 were allocated for expenditures other than

Table 10

ADJUSTED FARM AND NON-FARM DISTRIBUTION
OF FIXED CAPITAL INVESTMENT, 1952-57

| | Farm Investment[1] | | Non-Farm Investment[2] | |
	Value (million yuan)	Share (%)	Value (million yuan)	Share (%)
1952	3,775	45.8	4,478	54.2
1953	3,786	32.3	7,906	67.7
1954	3,899	27.7	10,180	72.3
1955	4,907	31.3	10,770	68.7
1956	7,634	33.2	15,356	66.8
1957	6,612	31.4	14,445	68.6
1952-57	30,613	32.6	63,135	67.4

Sources: 1. Appendix 1.
2. Deducting farm investment from total fixed capital investment.

food, fuel, clothing, and medical care. This unidentified item included expenditures for private housing construction, furniture, and
small farm implements, as well as expenses for weddings and
funerals.[26] The data in this survey would indicate that no peasant
household could afford 4.15 yuan per capita per year for housing
construction. It is more likely that they could spend only one-
third of this unidentified amount, or about 2 yuan a year. Adding
investment in collectively-owned buildings, per capita annual investment in rural housing would be around 2.5 to 3 yuan per year, which
comes very close to our estimates in Table 11.

Table 11

REVISED ESTIMATES FOR RURAL HOUSING INVESTMENT,
1952-57

	Total Rural Housing Investment	Rural Population	Per Capita Annual Investment
	(million yuan)	(million persons)	(yuan)
1952	1,180	503.19	2.3
1953	820	510.29	1.6
1954	1,240	520.17	2.3
1955	1,420	531.80	2.7
1956	2,660	538.65	4.9
1957	1,710	545.65	3.1
Average 1952-57			2.8

FOOTNOTES

1. T'ung-chi Kung-tso T'ung-hsün [Statistical Work Bulletin] (TCKTTH), No. 1, 1954, p. 2.

2. K. C. Yeh, "Capital Formation in Mainland China, 1931-36 and 1952-57" (unpublished dissertation, Columbia University), 1965, pp. 82-85; S. Ishikawa, National Income and Capital Formation in Mainland China: An Examination of Official Statistics (Tokyo: Institute of Asian Economic Affairs, 1965), pp. 99-108; and K. Chao, "Fixed Capital Investment in Communist China" op. cit. pp. 1-4.

3. Yueh Wei, "The Method of Computing National Income," Ching-chi Yen-chiu [Economic Research] No. 3, 1956, pp. 63-64.

4. For details, see First Five-Year Plan for Development of the National Economy of the People's Republic of China, 1953-1957. (Peking: Foreign Languages Press, 1956) pp. 28-29n.

5. W. W. Hollister, China's Gross National Product and Social Accounts, 1950-57 (New York: Free Press of Glencoe, 1958); Choh-ming Li, Economic Development of Communist China, (Berkeley and Los Angeles: University of California Press, 1959); Alexander Eckstein, The National Income of Communist China (New York: Free Press of Glencoe, 1961); and Ishikawa, op. cit.

6. A critical review of these studies has been made by K. C. Yeh, op. cit., pp. 124-142.

7. Ibid., p. 336.

8. "Data from the Typical Survey of the Distribution of Income in 228 Agricultural Producers' Cooperatives in 1957," T'ung-chi Yen-chiu [Statistical Research] No. 8, 1958, pp. 8-12.

9. Chao, op. cit., pp. 21-22.

10. Ibid., p. 21n.

11. Ibid., p. 42.

12. K. Chao, The Construction Industry in Communist China, (Chicago: Aldine, 1968), p. 213n.

13. This is clearly pointed out by the original source; see "Basic Situation of Construction Industry in Our Country," TCKTTH, No. 24, 1956, p. 31.

14. Ishikawa, op. cit., Table II-7, p. 122.

15. It is almost certain that state work for building and installations does not include work performed by the building enterprises owned by the supply and marketing cooperatives as well as the joint public-private building enterprises.

16. The reasons for including major repairs of machinery equipment and means of transportation in fixed capital investment have been elaborated in an article in TCKTTH, No. 15, 1956, pp. 19-20. According to this article, it is argued that since major repairs increase the remaining use value of fixed assets, they must be included in the total output of industry. However, major repairs must be distinguished from routine repairs, which are counted as a part of current production costs.

17. Fu Shih-hsin, "The Role of the Handicraft Industry in the National Economy," Ta-Kung-pao, July 1, 1959, p. 3.

18. Kuznets, op. cit., p. 34.

19. Ta-Chung Liu and Kung-Chia Yeh, The Economy of the Chinese Mainland, op. cit., App. I.

20. First Five-Year Plan, op. cit. p. 23.

21. Based on official investment data, Ishikawa estimated that of the total completed capital construction investment in 1953-57, building, installations and residential construction accounted for 71 percent, machinery, equipment and tools 27 percent and other investments 2 percent (Ishikawa, op. cit., p. 152). Since major repairs for machinery tend to be higher than major repairs for construction, in the absence of firm data, a proportion of 70:30 is assumed for the share of construction repairs and machinery repairs.

22. Total private construction investment is estimated at 4.35 billion yuan in 1953-55, while construction investment for private industry and joint public-private investment amounted to 610 million yuan for these three years. The proportion is 14%.

23. After nationalization of private industry in 1956-57, investment for private industry must decline. However, since the majority of private industrial enterprise was transformed into state-private joint enterprises, their investment still stood outside the state investment plan. As a result, the percent of private construction in the urban area remained very stable.

24. Chao I-wen, Hsin-chung-Kuo ti Kung-Yeh [New China's Industry] (Peking: T'ung-chi chu-pan-she, 1957), pp. 101-102.

25. In the same year, machine-building accounted for 50% of the metal-processing industry in the modern sector; see State Statistical Bureau, Wo-kuo Kang-tieh, Tien-li, Mei-t'an, Chi-hsieh, Fang-chih, Tsao-chih Kung-yeh ti Chin-hsi [The Present and Past of China's Iron and Steel, Electrical Power, Coal, Machinery, Textile and Paper Industries] (Peking: T'ung-chi Chu-pan-she), 1958, p. 120.

26. Yang Ying-chieh, A Report on a Survey of Five Agricultural Cooperatives and 600 Peasant Households (Peking: Tsai-cheng Ching-chi Chu-pan-she, 1958), pp. 40-42.

Chapter III

SECTORAL ALLOCATION OF FIXED
CAPITAL INVESTMENT

National income accounting in Mainland China is confined only
to five major sectors of the economy: industry, agriculture, building, trade, and transportation and communications. Both services
and administration are treated as "non-material producing sectors"
and are excluded from the national income accounts. [1]

However, in the allocation of capital investment the number
of economic sectors is increased to seven: (1) industry, (2) agriculture, (3) transportation and communications, (4) trade, banking,
and stockpiling, (5) culture, education and public health, (6) urban
public utilities, and (7) other. [2] Within this general classification
system, there are two different ways to define the sectors. The
first, in accordance with the technical function of the investment,
is called "functional classification." The second, in accordance
with the administrative agencies that control the enterprises in which
the investments are made, is called "administrative classification." [3]

When the First Five-Year Plan was formally published in 1955,
the sum of 42.74 billion yuan for investment in capital construction
was distributed in accordance with administrative classification. In
1959, a more detailed account based on a functional classification
divided the actual investment into eleven sectors. [4] Following the
administrative classification, we can regroup the official data for
actual investment into the same seven sectors as the planned investment. A comparison of these two sets of investment data is shown
in Table 12.

The allocations in Table 12 cover only capital investments in
the public sector and exclude private and cooperative investments.
As a result, they show a very samll percentage of investment in
the agricultural sector. During the 1953-57 period, state capital
investment allocated for agriculture, water conservation, forestry,
and meteorology accounted for only 8.2 percent of the total, or only
4.5 billion yuan. According to other official statements, private
investment in the agricultural sector during this period was between
10 and 17 billion yuan, of which 60 percent was for fixed capital
investment. [5]

Table 12

PLANNED AND ACTUAL DISTRIBUTION OF CAPITAL CONSTRUCTION
INVESTMENT IN THE FIRST FIVE-YEAR PLAN (IN MILLION YUAN)

Sector	Planned Investment[1]		Actual Investment[2]	
	Amount	Percentage of Total	Amount	Percentage of Total
Industry	24,850	58.2	30,800	56.0
Agriculture, water conservation, and forestry	3,260	7.6	4,510	8.2
Transportation and communication	8,210	19.2	10,285	18.7
Trade, banking, and stockpiling	1,280	3.0	2,140	3.9
Culture, education, and public health	3,080	7.2	4,455	8.1
Urban public utilities	1,600	3.7	1,440	2.6
Other	460	1.1	1,370	2.5
Total	42,740	100.0	55,000	100.0

Source: 1. First Five-Year Plan, p. 29.
         2. Ten Great Years, pp. 57-58.

It is quite evident that most of the private investment omitted in official data comes from agricultural cooperatives and peasant households. Since we have made a sizeable estimate of private farm investment, the distributive structure in Table 12 apparently cannot be directly applied to our estimated aggregate. However, if we deduct the state agricultural investment from total investment and compare the non-agricultural investment with our estimates for non-agricultural investment in Table 10, Chapter 2, it appears that the magnitudes of these two series are rather close. In the absence of a better alternative, we assume that official data on the distribution of fixed investment among various non-agricultural sectors is quite comprehensive and can be used as a basis to calculate distribution percentages in the non-agricultural sectors. The whole process of estimation involves four steps. First, from official statistics in Ten Great Years, we know the percentage distribution of capital construction investment among various. sectors during 1952-57.[6] Deducting agricultural investment from the total, we can derive non-agricultural investment. Second, taking non-agricultural investment as 100, we calculate the percentage distribution of the non-agricultural investment. Third, multiplying the percentage distribution of non-agricultural sectors to our estimated aggregate figure for non-agricultural sectors in Table 10, Chapter 2, we derive the investment in each of the non-agricultural sectors. Finally, adding our estimated investment for the agricultural sector to non-agricultural sectors we recalculate distribution for both agricultural and non-agricultural sectors. The results of these calculations are presented in absolute amounts and percentages in Table 13 while detailed accounts of the derivation are given in Appendix 2.

From Table 13, the distinctive patterns of the sectoral allocation of fixed capital investment during the first phase of industrialization in China stand out very clearly.

First, the lion's share of fixed investment went to industry, which accounted for 40 percent of the total. Its relative share rose from 29 percent in 1952 to 45 percent in 1957. In absolute terms, investment in industry almost quadrupled in five years. This clearly reflects the government's investment priority. Next came investment in agriculture. Although in absolute terms fixed investment in this sector doubled between 1952 and 1957, its relative share declined from 31 to only 23 percent. Moreover, the bulk of the fixed investment in this sector came from private sources; state investment accounted for only 38 percent of the total (Table 38, Chapter 5).

Table 13

ALLOCATION OF GROSS FIXED INVESTMENT BY ECONOMIC SECTOR, 1952-57

	(1) Agriculture	(2) Industry	(3) Transport	(4) M+ Sector (2)+(3)	(5) Dwellings	(6) Other services	(7) All services (5)+(6)
(I) Amount (in million yuan)							
1952	2,595	2,406	909	3,315	1,650	693	2,343
1953	2,966	3,976	1,170	5,146	1,617	1,963	3,580
1954	2,657	5,558	1,751	7,309	1,973	2,140	4,113
1955	3,487	6,333	2,176	8,509	1,994	1,687	3,681
1956	4,974	9,276	2,948	12,224	3,517	2,275	5,792
1957	4,902	9,578	2,368	11,946	2,375	1,834	4,209
1953-57	18,986	34,721	10,413	45,134	11,476	9,899	21,375
(II) Share (%)							
1952	31.4	29.1	11.2	40.3	20.0	8.3	28.3
1953	25.4	33.9	10.0	43.9	13.8	16.7	30.5
1954	18.8	39.5	12.4	51.9	14.0	15.2	29.2
1955	22.2	40.4	13.9	54.3	12.7	10.7	23.4
1956	21.6	40.4	12.8	53.2	15.3	9.9	25.2
1957	23.2	45.4	11.3	56.7	11.3	8.8	20.1
1953-57	22.2	40.6	12.2	52.8	13.4	11.6	25.0

Source: Appendix 2

The share of fixed investment for transportation and communications occupied 12 percent of the total. Although its absolute amount doubled between 1952 and 1957, the relative position of this sector remained rather stable.

Investment in housing construction accounted for 15 percent of the total. In absolute terms, the amount remained almost constant between 1953 and 1957; however, the sector's relative share declined steadily, from 22 percent in 1952 to only 11 percent in 1957. Also, 70 percent of the investment in housing construction occurred in the rural areas and was financed by private sources. State investment in urban housing appears to have been negligible (See Chapter 4).

Investment for all services (including housing) accounted for only one-fourth of the total. The share declined continuously from 1953, while the shares of agriculture and transportation and communications remained unchanged. Evidently, the regime diverted a larger share of resources to industrial investment at the expense of the service sector.

The distinctive features of investment policy in Mainland China will be clearer if data for other countries are given for comparison. Table 14 shows the distribution of fixed investment by economic sectors for the USSR in 1928-32, the USA in 1900-1912, and non-Communist countries grouped by per capita income in the 1950s.

China's allocation of fixed capital investment was quite similar to that of the Soviet Union during 1928-32. The share of investment in industry for these two countries was almost identical. While the share of investment in agriculture was slightly higher in China than in the USSR, China's proportion of investment in transport and communication was comparatively lower. Services in both countries registered a very low share. This illustrates that the two countries pursued similar development strategies during their respective First Five-Year Plan.

The differences in allocation patterns stand out clearly when Chinese data are compared with non-Communist countries.

First, the share of fixed capital investment channelled into industry in China far exceeded that share in other countries. On the other hand, China's share of fixed investment in transportation and communications was smaller.

Table 14

DISTRIBUTION OF GROSS FIXED INVESTMENT BY MAJOR SECTORS, MAINLAND CHINA AND OTHER SELECTED COUNTRIES (IN %)

Countries	(1) Agri-culture	(2) Industry	(3) Transport	(4) M+S (2)+(3)	(5) Dwelling	(6) Other	(7) All Services (5)+(6)
Mainland China, 1953-57[1]	22.2	40.6	12.2	52.8	14.8	10.2	25.0
USSR, 1928-32[2]	19.1	41.0	18.4	59.4	9.2	12.3	21.5
USA[3]							
1900-12	9.6	21.5	17.1	38.6	26.0	25.8	51.8
1920-40	5.3	25.0	14.7	39.7	19.0	34.0	55.0
Non-communist countries[4]							
High-income	7.8	30.0	14.9	44.9	21.5	25.7	47.2
Middle-income	13.2	28.4	15.2	44.1	24.2	17.9	42.1
Low-income	25.8	28.1	15.3	43.4	13.9	17.0	30.9

Sources: 1. Table 13.
2. Kaplan, "Capital Formation and Allocation," op.cit., pp. 52, 61.
3. Ibid., pp. 54, 61.
4. Kuznets, "Capital Formation Proportions," op. cit., p. 64. "Other services" includes government administration.

Second, the share of investment in agriculture in China was larger than in the high- and middle-income groups but smaller than in the low-income countries.

Third, the share of fixed investment in services in China appears to be very low compared with all non-communist countries.

The divergences reflect one salient feature of China's development strategy. In Western countries, economic development is associated with a rise in living standards. This is reflected in the high share of investment in the service sector, particularly in residential construction. In China, as in the case of the Soviet Union, emphasis has been placed on a high rate of growth. The share of investment in the industry plus transportation sector (M+) was much higher than in non-communist countries.

1. Sectoral Fixed Capital/Output Ratios

The salient features of sectoral allocation of fixed capital investment in China can be further gauged by comparing the sectoral distribution of gross output value. From national income estimates made by Liu and Yeh and the sectoral distribution of fixed capital investment as calculated in Table 13, we can derive ratio of share in fixed investment to share in domestic product for each economic sector.

The purpose of computing the gross sectoral fixed capital/output ratios is to observe the changes in economic structure in the process of industrialization. A sector ratio of less than 1 means that the share of fixed capital investment that this particular sector secures is smaller than the share it contributes to the gross domestic output. Conversely, if the sector ratio is more than 1, the sector secures a larger share of the country's fixed capital investment than it contributes to the country's domestic product. Since the very process of development involves changes in economic structure, which in turn means differential rates of growth among various sectors, such differential growth in turn is possible only if some sectors get larger investment allocations than others. The sectoral capital/output ratios therefore reflect the development policy of a country.

Based on national income data from Liu and Yeh's study, we derived the sectoral ratios for China. These are then compared with sectoral ratios for other countries in Table 15.

Table 15

SECTORAL FIXED CAPITAL/GROSS OUTPUT RATIOS,
MAINLAND CHINA AND OTHER SELECTED COUNTRIES

	(1) Agriculture	(2) Industry	(3) Transport	M+S (2)+(3)	(4) Services
I Share in total gross fixed investment (%)[1]					
China (1953-57)	22.2	40.6	12.2	52.8	25.0
Low-income countries	25.8	28.1	15.3	43.4	30.9
Middle-income countries	13.2	28.4	15.2	44.1	42.1
High-income countries	7.8	30.0	14.9	44.9	47.2
II Share in gross domestic product (%)					
China[2]	42.1	28.2	6.5	34.7	23.2
Low-income countries[3]	42.3	19.0	4.6	23.6	34.1
Middle-income countries[3]	24.4	31.3	6.1	37.4	36.2
High-income countries[3]	12.9	40.2	9.0	49.2	37.0
III Ratio of share in fixed investment to share in domestic product					
China	0.53	1.44	1.88	1.52	1.08
Low-income countries	0.61	1.48	3.33	1.85	0.91
Middle-income countries	0.54	0.91	2.49	1.13	1.16
High-income countries	0.60	0.75	1.51	0.90	1.28

Table 15 (con't)

Sources: 1. Table 14.
2. Liu-Yeh, op. cit., p. 213.
3. Kuznets, op. cit., pp. 37-40.

Table 15 shows a great disparity between the share of fixed investment and the share of gross output for various sectors in China. Despite strenuous efforts to convert the country from a predominantly agrarian economy into an industrial one, the structure of the domestic product remains similar to that of other low-income countries and strikingly different from the high-income group. During the First Plan period, agricultural output accounted for 42 percent of China's gross domestic product, compared to the 24 percent for middle-income countries and 13 percent for high-income countries.

While the existing output structure was unchanged, a larger proportion of the fixed capital investment was allocated to industry. Consequently, industry had a ratio larger than 1, while agriculture's ratio was lower than 1. China's ratio in the agricultural sector (0.53) was the lowest almong all countries compared. This would mean that the share of capital investment allocated to agriculture as compared to the GNP share of agriculture was relatively lower in China than in other countries, including underdeveloped countries. On the other hand, the M+ sector in China received a much larger share of fixed investment than its contribution to gross domestic product. Since for a given period, additions to reproducible capital stock usually are associated with additions to output, the continuous outflow of capital from agriculture to the M+ sector brought about a rapid growth of industry and a near stagnation of agricultural output. The lack of feedback to the agricultural sector widened the disparity between agriculture and industry and finally halted the further advancement of the M+ sector as a whole.

2. Sectoral Incremental Capital/Output Ratios

The ratios of sectoral contributions to gross product to their share of fixed capital investment disclose some special features of allocation policy. They do not tell us how this allocation policy affected the rate of growth. In this section, we want to advance a step further and explore the association between incremental output and the cumulated gross fixed investment for various economic sectors, that is, to calculate the sectoral incremental capital/output ratios.

By incremental capital/output ratios, we mean the ratios between additions to reproducible fixed capital stock and additions to output. To calculate these, we need data on changes in both domestic product and the product originated by each industrial sector. In addition, we need data on the distribution of fixed capital investment among the same sectors. The denominator of the ratio must reflect changes in real product (output expressed in constant prices), while the numerator is the fixed capital investment over the interval covered by the changes in product. Usually, there is a time lag between an increment in capital and an increment in output. In Table 16, the sectoral incremental capital/output ratios (ICOR) in the Chinese economy are based on the ratio of cumulated fixed capital investment during 1952-56 and the output increment in 1952-57. The output data are from Liu and Yeh's national income study with modifications in sectoral classification. Adjustment was also made to distribute the annual total depreciation charge to each sector for the purpose of deriving sectoral gross output value. The cumulated fixed investments are calculated on both a gross and a net basis. Conceptually, the net capital/output ratio is more relevant to the study of economic growth because it is the addition to, not the replacement of, capital stock which has the most direct bearing on net addition to product. However, the estimation of capital depreciation and consumption is fraught with many difficulties. Since the net fixed investments in Table 16 are derived from fragmentary data, the gross capital investment estimates are probably more reliable.

The over-all net incremental capital/output ratio for the Chinese economy as a whole during 1952-57 was quite similar to that for other low-income countries (Table 17). However, the gross incremental capital/output ratio in China was close to that for the middle-income countries but lower than those for both low-income and high-income countries, which suggests that the depreciation rate probably was much lower in China than in other underdeveloped countries. In China, the average depreciation rate of fixed assets in all departments of the national economy was estimated as 1.4 percent in 1952, 2.4 in 1953, 2.4 in 1954, and 2.8 percent in 1955.[7] This means that the depreciation term ranged from 35 to more than 71 years. These low depreciation rates for China reduced the difference between the net and gross ICOR.

However, except for agriculture, the sectoral incremental capital/output ratios were lower for China than for other low-income countries (Table 18). The sectoral ICOR in industry was about 30 percent below the low-income country average and as a result was almost equal to that in the middle income countries. At first sight, one might draw the implication from these low ICOR's that Chinese industry operated on a highly labor-intensive basis and/or she had a much higher efficiency in the use of capital. But neither of these

Table 16

SECTORAL INCREMENTAL CAPITAL/OUTPUT RATIOS, 1952–57

Sectors	(1) Incremental output, 1952-57, in net value-added (million yuan) GNP	(1) NNP	(2) Cumulated gross fixed invest- ment, 1952-56 (million yuan)	(3) Cumulated net fixed invest- ment, 1952-56 (million yuan)	(4) ICOR Gross (2) GNP	(4) ICOR Net (3) NNP
Whole Economy	26,150	23,930	72,690	52,270	2.8	2.2
Agriculture	3,970	2,970	16,680	7,510	4.2	2.5
Industry	15,460	14,990	27,550	23,200	1.8	1.5
Transportation and Communi- cations	1,790	1,500	8,950	6,160	5.0	4.1
Other	4,930	4,470	19,510	15,400	3.9	3.4

Source: Appendix 3

Table 17

NET AND GROSS INCREMENTAL CAPITAL/OUTPUT RATIOS
MAINLAND CHINA AND OTHER SELECTED COUNTRIES

	Net ICOR	Gross ICOR
China[1]	2.2	2.8
Low-income countries[2]	2.3	3.4
Middle-income countries[2]	1.8	2.9
High-income countries[2]	5.27	6.3

Sources: 1. Table 16.
2. Kuznets, op. cit., pp. 58, 64.

Table 18

SECTORAL GROSS INCREMENTAL CAPITAL/OUTPUT RATIOS
MAINLAND CHINA AND OTHER COUNTRIES

| Sectors | China 1953-57 | USSR 1928-32 | Non-communist countries | | |
			Low-income countries	Middle-income countries	High-income countries
Whole economy	2.8	4.8	3.4	2.9	6.3
Agriculture	4.2	-	2.9	2.8	11.0
Industry	1.8	-	2.4	1.7	3.2
Transportation and communications	5.0	-	8.3	8.2	7.0
Other	3.9	-	4.2	8.0	11.7

Sources: China from Table 16; USSR from Kaplan, op. cit., p. 52; other countries from Kuznets, op. cit., p. 64.

hypotheses can be really validated. As is well known, at least during the FFYP Chinese planners exhibited a strong preference for large plants and for capital-intensive techniques. More than 85 percent of the capital investment in industry during this period went into 694 large industrial projects equipped with modern machinery. It is doubtful too that this phenomenon can be explained on efficiency grounds. The rather puzzling phenomenon can be explained by looking into the share of industry in both the incremental output and the cumulated fixed capital investment.

In 1952-57, of the total increment of output, 62.7 percent was contributed by the industrial sector. But industry absorbed only 37.9 percent of the cumulated gross fixed investment and 44.4 percent of the cumulated net fixed investment. Since the share of industry in the total incremental output far exceeds its share in the cumulated investment, industry naturally has a low ICOR. And since industrial output accounted for a colossal portion of the total incremental output, the ICOR for the whole economy was also scaled down.

Apart from reasons noted above, there are at least three sets of factors which have caused the low ICOR in Chinese industry.

First, the period under study was a continuation of the economic recovery of 1949-52. Until 1956, a huge portion of industrial output was contributed by existing facilities rather than by newly built plants. According to official statistics, existing production capacity contributed the following percentages to current industrial output: 74 percent in 1954, 75 in 1955, 66 in 1956 and 70 percent in 1957.[8] This suggests that there were sizeable unutilized industrial facilities at the beginning of the First Plan, which enabled China to achieve a high rate of growth in industry with less capital input.

Second, with the advent of large-scale industrialization in 1953, strenuous efforts were made to expand technical manpower. The total number of engineers and technicians rose from 164,000 in 1952 to 449,000 in 1957, an increase of 180 percent.[9] The rate of increase in technical manpower was more than twice that for all industrial workers (80 percent). Thus the industrial labor force contained an increasing proportion of technical manpower. The emphasis on human capital was also demonstrated by the sharp rise in state outlays for education and scientific research. State expenditures for education at all levels increased from 813 million yuan in 1951 to 2,906 million yuan in 1957, a 3.5-fold jump.[10] The growth of technical manpower and the acceleration of research and development undoubtedly promoted labor productivity and thus enhanced the efficiency of capital.

Third, since the denominator of the ICOR is the industrial output value expressed in 1952 constant prices, any upward bias in the valuation would press down the ICOR. It is well known that the official gross output data valued at 1952 constant prices overstated the value of industrial products, particularly capital goods. This imparts an upward bias into the official statistics on industrial output. Furthermore, official prices have overvalued most of the new industrial products, which usually grew faster than industrial output as a whole. [11] For all these reasons, there is a built-in upward bias in the official industrial output value data. The Liu-Yeh estimates of industrial output were based on official data without correction for these biases. Consequently, the denominator is inflated.

FOOTNOTES

1. Research Office, State Statistical Bureau, "A Preliminary Study of the Production and Distribution of our National Income," T'ung-Chi Yen-Chiu (January 1958), pp. 11-15.

2. First Five-Year Plan, p. 29.

3. Some examples may be cited to clarify the differences. For instance, under the functional classification, all investment in industrial enterprises is treated as industrial investment; but under the administrative classification, only investment in those enterprises under the control of industrial ministries is counted as industrial investment. Investment in industrial enterprises under the control of ministries of railways, transportation, or culture is counted as investment in that department.

4. The 11 sectors are: 1. industry, 2. building, 3. prospecting for natural resources, 4. agriculture, forestry, water conservation and meteorology, 5. transport and communications, 6. trade, 7. culture, education and scientific research, 8. public health, 9. urban public utilities, 10, government bureau, and 11. others. Official explanations denote that in accordance with the administrative classification, both building and prospecting for natural resources are included in industry, while culture, education, scientific research, public health and welfare are combined into a more broad sector called "culture, education and public health." Ten Great Years, pp. 57-60.

5. Wang Kuang-wei, "Strengthen Industry's Aid to Agriculture," Hung-ch'i [Red Flag], No. 16, 1959.

6. Ten Great Years, pp. 57-60.

7. Sun Yeh-fang, "Discussion on Gross Output Value and Other Topics," T'ung-chi Kung-tso, No. 13, 1957.

8. C. M. Li, ed., Industrial Development in Communist China (New York: Praeger, 1964), p. 19.

9. Chu-yuan Cheng, Scientific and Engineering Manpower in Communist China 1949-63 (Washington, D.C.: National Science Foundation, 1966), pp. 111-112.

10. *Ibid.*, pp. 80-81.

11. For details, see Chu-yuan Cheng, *The Machine-Building Industry in Communist China*, *op. cit.*, pp. 68-71.

Chapter IV

THE BRANCH ALLOCATION OF FIXED INVESTMENT
IN NON-AGRICULTURAL SECTORS

The sectoral allocation of fixed investment provides us with
some useful insights into the general direction of China's development strategy. However, for the purpose of studying the structure
of fixed investment, sectoral distribution is probably still too
aggregative. For instance, the industrial sector includes more
than ten branches, which vary in their contribution to national income
and in their significance for economic growth. The distribution
of investment among these various industrial branches usually
has a direct consequence for the growth of industry as a whole. In
general, a higher share of fixed investment in heavy or basic capital goods industries is always associated with a higher rate of growth
in the industrial sector. To compare the investment patterns of
two economies, we need to know not merely the sectoral variations
but also the branch differences within the major sectors.

In this chapter, we will focus our attention on the allocation
of fixed investment among the branches of the non-agricultural
sectors. The branches of particular interest are (1) major
branches of industry, (2) railway construction, and (3) housing
construction. The branch distribution within the agricultural
sector will be discussed in the following chapter.

(1) Branch Distribution of Investment in Industry

In the Chinese planning and statistical system, the industrial
sector consists of fourteen branches. Under the broad heading of
"heavy industry" there are nine branches: iron and steel, non-
ferrous metals, electric power, coal, petroleum, metal-processing,
chemicals, building materials, and lumber. Belonging to "light
industry" are such branches as textiles, food-processing, drugs and
medical supplies, paper-making, and other light industry.[1] Despite
this classification, in the First Five-Year Plan, total basic
construction investment for industry was allocated among nine broad
branches corresponding to the central ministries who exercise direct
control over the investment. This distribution pattern is shown in
Table 19.

Table 19

DISTRIBUTION OF PLANNED CAPITAL CONSTRUCTION INVESTMENT
IN THE INDUSTRIAL SECTOR UNDER THE
FIRST FIVE-YEAR PLAN, BY MINISTRIES

Ministry	Investment (million yuan)	Percentages of total
Heavy industry	6,490	24.4
Fuel industry	6,790	25.5
Machine-building	6,930	26.0
Textiles	1,160	4.4
Light Industry	690	2.6
Geology	200	0.8
Building industry[1]	690	2.6
Local industry	1,900	7.1
Non-industrial ministries[2]	1,770	6.6
Total	26,620	100.0

Source: The First Five Year Plan, p. 30.

Notes: 1. Including local building enterprises.
2. This refers to the capital invested by the
ministries of Commerce and Food in the
processing industry, by the ministries
Railways and Communications in enterprises
for maintenance of locomotives, vehicles,
and ships, and in their building projects,
by the ministry of Cultural Affairs in the
film industry, etc. (This figure was not
included in the total for the industrial
sector given in Table 12, Chapter 3).

Since the jurisdiction of each ministry has changed frequently, classification by industrial ministries apparently would not be meaningful over a longer span of time. Moreover, the jurisdictions of industrial ministries in China differ considerably from those in other countries, and statistics based on such classifications cannot be used for international comparison.[2] Thus, although the data in Table 19 provide the most complete available account of investment distribution among various branches, they are not suitable for our purpose.

From widely scattered sources, capital investment for twelve of the fourteen industrial branches can be gathered; they are presented in Table 20. Since the data are piecemeal rather than of a more systematic nature, the twelve branches here do not exhaust all investment in the industrial sector. Moreover, the data in Table 19 include investments in local industry and industrial investment made by non-industrial ministries. The figures in Table 20 are for investment in enterprises under the control of central industrial ministries alone. Consequently the total investment given in Table 20 is smaller than that in Table 19. The difference equals the investment made by local industries and non-industrial ministries. Since both investments in local industries and in non-industrial ministries are expressed in lump sums (see Table 19), and since the remaining amount in Table 19 is equal to the total in Table 20, we are on safe ground in asserting that they both refer to the same planned investment in the industrial sector during the First Five-Year Plan period.

Although Table 20 presents a fairly complete picture of the distribution among various industrial branches, it has a major defect. Official sources have explicitly noted that these are planned targets. They are bound to differ from actual investment. For our purposes, it is the actual rather than the planned investment that is more relevant. Unfortunately, because of the extreme paucity of data on actual investment among various branches, we are unable to construct a similar distribution pattern for actual investment. As a result, we are compelled to use the data in Table 20 for our analysis. To justify this decision we must figure out the degree of deviation between distribution patterns in the planned investment and in the actual investment.

From scattered sources we have collected actual investment for four major industries--electric power, iron and steel, metal-

Table 20

DISTRIBUTION OF PLANNED CAPITAL INVESTMENT
IN THE INDUSTRIAL SECTOR, 1953-57,
BY MAJOR BRANCHES (OFFICIAL DATA)

Branches	Investment (million yuan)	Percentage
1. Iron and Steel	2,929	12.8
2. Building Materials	380	1.7
3. Chemical[1]	(3,181)	(13.9)
4. Non-ferrous Metal[1]		
5. Coal	2,970	12.9
6. Petroleum	702	3.1
7. Electric Power	2,674	11.6
8. Metal-Processing	3,413	14.9
9. (Defense Industry)[2]	(3,517)	(15.3)
10. Textile	1,240	5.4
11. Food Processing	496	2.2
12. Paper-Making[3]	380	1.7
13. Others[4]	1,083	4.5
Total[5]	22,965	100.0

Sources and Notes: Except as noted, all figures are
from Chao I-wen, Hsing-chung-kuo
ti Kung-Yeh [Industry in New China],
Peking: T'ung-chi Ch'u-pan-she,
1957, pp. 39-57.

1. From Table 19, investment for "Heavy
Industry Ministry" is 6,490 million
yuan. This amount covers iron and
steel, building materials, non-ferro
metals, and chemicals. Since in-

Sources and Notes for Table 20 (continued):

vestments for the first two industries
are given, the residual must be investment
in the last two industries.

2. From the Table 19 investment for ministries
of machine-building is set at 6,930 million
yuan. The difference between this total
and the figure in line 8 (3,413 million
yuan) is assumed to be investment in the
defense industry, mainly for the second
ministry of machine-building.

3. Present and Past, p. 205.

4. This is derived as a residual. Included
in this branch are such industries as
light industry, drugs and medical supplies
and lumber.

5. Present and Past, p. 39.

processing, and textiles--during the four-year period from 1953
to 1956. Using these data, we have computed the share of actual
investment in each of these four industries and compared it with
their respective shares in the planned investment. The results,
shown in Table 21, indicate that the share of actual investment in
electric power, iron and steel and metal-processing fell short of
their shares in the planned investment. Total share for these
three branches was 2 percentage points less than their planned
investment (36.7 percent, instead of 38.8 percent). Conversely,
the textile industry's share of actual investment rose by 0.7 percentage points. Since the total share of actual investment for these
four known branches is 1.4 percentage points lower than their
planned investment, some other branches must have enhanced their
position. But in general, the distortion can be classed as insignif-
icant. This would suggest that Table 20 still represents the best
approximation of the branch distribution of fixed investment in the
Chinese industry during the First Five-Year Plan period.

Basing on the percentage distribution in Table 20 and the total
fixed investment for industrial sector as estimated in Table 13,
Chapter III, distribution of fixed capital investment by industrial
branches can be calculated (Table 22). In Table 22, it is quite
evident that the bulk of Chinese industrial investment during the
First Plan period was over-whelmingly concentrated in six branches:
iron and steel, chemicals, non-ferrous metals, coal, electric power,
and metal-processing. Altogether, they accounted for more than
80 percent of the total. Clearly, the priority of development in the
first phase of Chinese industrialization was placed on fuel, metals,
and metal-processing--a pattern exactly in agreement with the
typical scheme of forced industrialization.

Compared with the investment distribution in Japan in 1956,
the year data are available, and in the Soviet Union in 1929-32,
the Chinese allocation shows a great similarity to the Soviet
pattern but is widely divergent from the Japanese. As can be seen
from Table 23, the investment share for iron and steel in China
was close to that in the Soviet Union in 1932 but far exceeded that
in Japan in 1956. The investment share for fuel industries (coal,
petroleum, and electric power) was 27.6 percent in China, almost
identical with that in the Soviet Union in 1929 (27.9 percent)--
although China concentrated on coal and electric power while the
Soviet Union paid more attention to petroleum. For the consumer
goods industries--textiles, food, and paper-making--the Chinese

Table 21

COMPARISON OF PLANNED AND ACTUAL INVESTMENT IN FOUR INDUSTRIES,
1953-57 (IN MILLION YUAN)

	1953	1954	1955	1956	1957	1953-56	1953-57
(1) Planned investment							
Total	2,831	3,564	4,686	5,670	6,204	16,761	22,965
Electric power[2]	255.3	343.6	565.3	707.9	801	1,873	2,674
Iron and steel[3]	300	282	630	833	883	2,046	2,929
Metal-processing[4]	455	614	785	789	770	2,643	3,413
Textiles[5]	220	348	197	291	184	1,056	1,240
(2) Actual investment							
Total[6]	2,840	3,830	4,300	6,820	7,240	17,790	25,030
Electric power[2]	262	392	535	724	944	1,913	2,857
Iron and steel[7]			2,060			2,060	
Metal-processing[7]			2,550			2,550	
Textiles[5]			1,250			1,250	
(3) Relative share							
Electric industry							
Planned	9.0	9.7	12.0	12.5	13.0	11.1	11.6
Actual	9.0	10.2	12.4	10.6	13.0	10.8	11.4
Iron and Steel							
Planned	10.5	7.9	13.4	14.6	14.2	12.0	12.8
Actual						11.6	
Metal-processing							
Planned	16.0	17.2	16.7	13.9	12.4	15.7	14.9
Actual						14.3	
Textiles							
Planned	7.7	9.7	4.2	5.1	2.9	6.3	5.4
Actual						7.0	

Table 21 (cont'd)

Sources for Table 21:
1. Present and Past, p. 14.
2. Ibid., p. 54.
3. Ibid., p. 14.
4. Ibid., p. 116.
5. Ibid., p. 159.
6. Ten Great Years, p. 57.
7. Chi-hua Ching-chi, [Planned Economy], No. 9, 1957, p. 13.

Table 22

DISTRIBUTION OF ESTIMATED FIXED CAPITAL INVESTMENT
IN INDUSTRIAL SECTOR, 1953-57
BY MAJOR BRANCHES
(MILLION YUAN)

Branches	Investment	Percentage
Iron and steel	4,444	12.8
Building materials	591	1.7
Chemical Non-ferrous metal }	4,826	13.9
Coal	4,479	12.9
Petroleum	1,076	3.1
Electric power	4,028	11.6
Metal-processing	5,173	14.9
Defense industry	5,312	15.3
Textile	1,875	5.4
Food processing	764	2.2
Paper-making	591	1.7
Others	1,562	4.5
Total	34,721	100.0

Sources: For Total: From Table 13, Chapter 3.

For Percentage: From Table 20.

Table 23

COMPARISON OF FIXED INVESTMENT ALLOCATION
IN MAINLAND CHINA, JAPAN, AND THE SOVIET
UNION, BY SELECTED INDUSTRIAL BRANCHES (%)

	Mainland China (1953-57)[1]	USSR (1929)[2]	(1932)[2]	Japan (1956)[3]
Iron and steel	12.8	10.1	13.6	8.4
Metal-processing and machine-building	30.2	n.a.	n.a.	13.7
Non-ferrous metals	13.9	3.5	5.2	2.1
Chemicals		n.a.	n.a.	17.1
Electric power	11.6	9.6	6.9	20.4
Coal	12.9	8.8	7.5	2.9
Petroleum	3.1	9.5	4.3	10.3
Textiles	5.4			10.3
Food processing	2.2	18.2	9.8	5.1
Paper-making	1.7			6.2
Other	6.4			13.8

(The figure 13.9 in the Mainland China column spans both the Non-ferrous metals and Chemicals rows.)

Sources: 1. Table 20.
2. Kaplan, "Capital Formation and Allocation," op. cit., p. 66.
3. These percentages are derived from
Miyohei Shinohara, "Capital Formation
in Post-War Japan, A Statistical
Evaluation," in Asian Studies in Income
and Wealth (Bombay: Asia Publishing
House, 1965), p. 128. His figures have
been regrouped so as to make the data
comparable to data on Mainland China.

share (9.3 percent) was much lower than that in the Soviet Union in 1929 but much closer to that in 1932 (9.8 percent).

Compared with Japan in 1956, China's investment was less balanced between capital and consumer goods. In Japan, the ratio between these two broad sectors was roughly 75:25 while in China, it was 87:13.[3] Moreover, Japan's shares for iron and steel and metal-processing also were much smaller than in China. This might indicate that Japanese industry in 1956 not only enjoyed a more balanced development among various branches, but also was more consumer oriented.

One significant factor which might account for the divergence between Japan and China lies in the difference in the stage of development of these two economies. While China in the early 1950s was only at the take-off stage, Japan in 1956 was already a mature industrial economy.

China's investment policy in industry can be further gauged by calculating the ratio of investment in metals and metal-processing industries to investment in all manufacturing. The numerator of this ratio includes investments for steel and iron and for metal-processing (including machine-building). The denominator includes investment in all manufacturing industries but excludes mining and electric power. The results compared with Japan, the USSR, and the United States can be seen in Table 24.

Table 24 reveals two distinctive patterns of investment in industry. In the two Communist countries, an extremely high proportion of industrial investment was accorded to the metals and metal products industries. In the three non-Communist countries, the proportion is much lower. The proportion in India was higher than Japan but lower than China. The Chinese ratio during 1953-57 was slightly higher than that in the USSR in 1928-38 and was almost as high as that in the United States during World War II (1940-45). The fact that China devoted more than half of her manufacturing investment to the metal and metal products industries clearly reflects the Chinese leaders' determination to achieve self-sufficiency in capital goods within a very short span of time.

2. Investment in Railways

Among the non-agricultural sectors, transportation and

Table 24

RATIOS OF INVESTMENT IN METALS AND METAL PRODUCTS
INDUSTRIES TO INVESTMENT IN ALL MANUFACTURING,
MAINLAND CHINA, JAPAN, THE SOVIET UNION,
AND THE UNITED STATES

China[1]

(1953-57)   56.7

Japan[2]

(1956)   32.8

USSR[3]

(1928-35)   49.6

(1928-38)   52.6

(1928-40)   49.0

United States[3]

(1904-09)   35.2

(1909-14)   33.8

(1914-19)   36.3

(1940-45)   58.5

(1947)   34.8

India[4]

(1951-56)   47.9

Sources: 1. Calculated from Table 20.
          2. Calculated from Miyohei Shinohara, op.
              cit., p. 128.
          3. Kaplan, op. cit., p. 63.
          4. V. V. Bhatt, "Savings and Capital Forma-
              tion," Economic Development and Cultural
              Change, Vol. VII, No. 3, Ap. 1959, p. 333.

Table 25

OFFICIAL DATA ON RAILWAY INVESTMENT, 1952-57
(MILLION YUAN)

	(1) Total capital construction investment[1]	(2) Investment in transportation and communications[1]		(3) Investment in railways[1]		(4) Railways as percent of transportation and communications
		Amount	%	Amount	%	
1952	4,360	760	17.5	510	11.6	66.3
1953	8,000	1,070	13.4	650	8.1	60.5
1954	9,070	1,500	16.5	950	10.4	63.5
1955	9,300	1,760	19.0	1,220	13.2	70.0
1956	14,800	2,610	17.7	1,760	11.9	67.2
1957	13,830	2,070	15.0	1,340	9.7	64.7
1953-57	55,000	9,010	16.4[2]	5,920	10.8	65.9

Sources: 1. Ten Great Years, p. 58.
2. This is calculated on functional basis. On an administrative basis the five-year average would be 18.7 percent. Ibid., p. 59.

Table 26

SHARE OF RAILWAY INVESTMENT IN TOTAL
PUBLIC AND PRIVATE FIXED INVESTMENT, 1952-57
(IN MILLION YUAN)

	Total fixed investment[1]	Investment in transportation and communications[1]	Investment in railways[2]	Percentage of total fixed investment	
				Transportation and communications	Railway
1952	8,253	909	603	11.2	7.4
1953	11,692	1,170	708	10.1	6.1
1954	14,079	1,751	1,112	12.4	7.9
1955	15,677	2,176	1,523	13.9	9.7
1956	22,990	2,948	1,981	12.8	8.6
1957	23,057	2,368	1,532	11.3	5.3
1953-57	85,495	10,413	6,856	12.2	8.0

Sources: 1. Table 13, Chapter III.
2. Column 4 of Table 25 multiplied by column 2 of this table.

communications ranked second in investment, although its share
was only one-third that of industry. According to official statistics,
this sector absorbed 18.7 percent of the total government capital
construction investment.[4] When the private investments in housing
and other rural investment are included in the total, the share of
transportation and communications drops to only 12.2 percent de-
noting that social-overhead capital in China was rather meager
during the First Five-Year Plan.

Since the amount of investment in the whole transportation and
communications sector was limited, railroad investment was also
rather lean. Official statistics show that during the First Plan
only one-tenth of capital construction investment in the public
sector went to railway construction (Table 25). This proportion
decreases to only 8 percent when private investment is included in
the investment total (Table 26).

Compared with the USSR and United States, China's investment
in railways was rather low (Table 27). In the Soviet First Plan
period, the share of investment going to railway construction was
13 percent, while in the initial period of industrialization in the
United States, the share was as high as 21.5 percent (1880-1890).
In the thirty-year span between 1880 and 1912, the United States
devoted roughly 16 percent of its capital investment to railways.

Table 27

PERCENTAGE OF RAILWAY INVESTMENT IN TOTAL INVESTMENT,
CHINA, USSR, AND THE UNITED STATES

China[1]		USSR[2]		USA[2]	
1952	7.4	1928/29-32	12.7	1880-1890	21.5
1953-57	8.0	1933-37	12.4	1890-1900	17.5
		1938-42 (planned)	12.9	1900-1912	13.0
		1946-50 (planned)	16.0	1880-1912	16.0

Sources: 1. Table 26.
2. Kaplan, op. cit., p. 60.

The low ratio of railway investment to total investment
is rather unique. In most advanced countries, industrialization was
preceded, virtually without exception, by a substantial build-up of
transportation and other forms of social overhead capital. As
Rostow pointed out, the most important functions of such investment
have been to reduce transport costs within the economy to permit
resources to be cheaply and efficiently combined, to enlarge the
domestic market, and to make possible the efficient conduct of
foreign trade.[5] In the Chinese case, transportation did not receive
substantial investment. Railway construction, which was the
initial leading sector in many countries, was not so important in
China.

3. Investment in Housing

In Chinese official statistics, residential construction did not
appear as an independent sector of capital construction investment.
It was treated as a component of the "other sectors." One official
source gave the volume of residential investment for the three years
from 1954 to 1956. Using these data and the annual data on the
total floor space of residential construction, we can derive figures
for investment in housing within the state plan (Table 28).

Figures in Table 28 are for state investment only and exclude
private housing construction in rural areas. According to our
estimate in Chapter II, total rural housing investment was more
than twice the housing investment under the state plan. Total
housing investment during the 1952-57 period is summarized in
Table 29.

With the addition of private housing in rural areas, the
share of housing in total fixed investment amounted to 13.4 percent
in the First Plan period (1953-57). This proportion is much
higher than that in the USSR between 1928-32, but much lower than
in the USA in 1880 to 1929 (Table 30).

Table 28

INVESTMENT IN RESIDENTIAL CONSTRUCTION WITHIN THE STATE PLAN 1952-57
(IN MILLION YUAN)

	(1) Total building & installation	(2) Residential	(3) Non-Residential[4]
1952	2,578	470[2]	2,108
1953	4,896	797[2]	4,099
1954	5,138	733[3]	4,405
1955	5,074	574[3]	4,500
1956	8,559	857[3]	7,702
1957	7,736	665[2]	7,071
1953-57	31,403	3,626	27,777

Sources: 1. State Statistical Bureau, Communique 1956, and "Communique on the Final Results of the Implementation of the First Five-Year Plan."

2. Extrapolated on the basis of figures for 1954-56 (see note 3 below), and on the annual data on the total floor space of residential construction given in Ten Great Years, p. 217.

3. Chai Mao-chou, "Our Method of Forecasting the Implementation of Investment Plans," T'ung-chi Kung-tso, No. 4, 1957, p. 16.

4. Residuals.

Table 29

TOTAL INVESTMENT IN HOUSING CONSTRUCTION, 1952-57
(IN MILLION YUAN)

	Investment within state plan[1]	Imputed rural housing investment[2]	Total housing investment	Housing as % of total fixed investment[3]
1952	470	1,180	1,650	20.0
1953	797	820	1,617	13.8
1954	733	1,240	1,973	14.0
1955	574	1,420	1,994	12.7
1956	857	2,660	3,517	15.3
1957	665	1,710	2,375	11.3
1953-57	3,626	7,850	11,476	13.4

Sources: 1. Table 28
2. Table 11, Chapter II.
3. Computed from investment totals in Table 10, Chapter II.

Table 30

PERCENTAGE OF HOUSING CONSTRUCTION IN TOTAL INVESTMENT,
CHINA, USSR, AND THE UNITED STATES

China[1]		USSR[2]		United States[2]	
1953-57	13.4	1928-29-32	9.2	1880-90	29.6
		1933-37	9.1	1900-12	26.0
		1938-42 (plan)	8.2	1920-29	24.6
		1946-50 (plan)	16.9	1930-40	13.5

Sources: 1. Table 29.
2. Kaplan, op. cit., p. 61.

4. Conclusions

The foregoing analysis permits us to draw a few conclusions about the rationale underlying China's allocation of fixed investment among the various branches in the non-agricultural sectors.

Within the industrial sector, the Chinese decision to concentrate the overwhelming portion of fixed investment in the basic industries, especially steel, coal, electrical power, and metal-processing, may arise not only from the commitment to a forced drafted industrialization program, but also partly from the constraint of agricultural production. As is well-known, the development of consumer goods industries not only is conditioned by the amount of capital investment, but also, and more significantly, is restrained by the supply of raw materials. Since 80-90 percent of the raw materials used by consumer goods industries are supplied by the agricultural sector, the expansion of the consumer goods branch is bound to be rather limited as long as agriculture was accorded a low development priority. During the First Five-Year Plan period, with a lag in agricultural output, a portion of productive capacity in consumer goods industries was kept idle. By 1957, the rates of utilization of capacity in major consumer goods industries were as follows: 85 percent for textiles, 66 percent for sugar-making,

75 percent for oil-pressing, 52 percent for tobacco rolling, 68 percent for flour mills, 69 percent for leather, and 53 percent for the can industry.[6] As long as the bottleneck for consumer goods industries comes from raw materials rather than from capacity, it seems quite reasonable for the Chinese planners to concentrate their investment funds in the capital goods industries.

The low ratio of investment in railway transportation may stem from the fact that China possesses a huge labor force in the old-fashioned transportation sector. In 1957, total employment in traditional transportation was estimated at 10 million persons.[7] The existence of such a huge labor force in traditional transport enabled China to reduce its investment in modern transport without a bottleneck serious enough to put a brake on industrial development.

Moreover, transportation and housing investments are characterized by such properties as a long period of gestation and exceptional durability. Consequently, the capital/output ratio is often exceedingly high in these two sectors. Experiences in Canada in 1950 and in the United States in 1939 show that the capital/output ratio in transport and communications was roughly five times that in secondary manufacturing.[8] The allocation of a sizeable portion of investment to transportation and housing may slow down the rate of growth in the short run. If manufacturing is to make some headway before investment in social overhead becomes heavy, the pressure on capital would be much less. It is probably this consideration that caused a smaller share of fixed investment to be allocated to transportation and other social-overhead sectors during China's First Five-Year Plan.

FOOTNOTES

1. Fan Wei-chung, <u>Ti-i Ko Wu-nien Chi-hua Chieh-sho</u> [Explanation of the First Five-Year Plan] (Peking: Kung-jen Chu-pan she, 1955), p. 27.

2. For example, in China electric power is considered a part of the fuel industry, while in Japan it is a part of public utilities.

3. <u>Ten Great Years,</u> p. 61.

4. This is calculated on administrative basis. On functional basis, the percentage would be 16.4 percent. <u>Ten Great Years,</u> p. 59.

5. W. W. Rostow (ed.), <u>The Economics of Take-off into Sustained Growth</u> (New York: St. Martin's Press, 1965), p. 17.

6. <u>Hsueh-hsi</u> [Study], Peking, No. 20, 1957.

7. Liu-Yeh, <u>op. cit.</u>, p. 597.

8. In the United States in 1939, the capital/output ratio for transport was 2.55, compared with 0.55 for secondary manufacturing; in Canada in 1950, the capital/output ratio for transport was 8.15, against 1.69 for secondary manufacturing. See A. K. Cairncross, "Capital Formation in the Take-off," in Rostow, <u>op. cit.</u>, p. 256.

Chapter V

ALLOCATION OF FIXED CAPITAL INVESTMENT
WITHIN THE AGRICULTURAL SECTOR

As we have noted, state investment in agriculture was rather meagre during the First Five Year Plan. Of the total planned state capital construction investment only 7.6 percent was devoted to the agricultural sector.[1] In chapter II we estimated a sizeable amount of private investment in the rural areas. In this chapter we want to examine the structure of the fixed investment in the total agricultural sector, including both public and private investments. Theoretically, investments in the rural area include housing construction, modern and old fashioned implements, livestock and carts, water conservation, reclamation, and other miscellaneous investments. Since we have treated residential housing as an independent sector, housing construction is excluded from our discussion of rural investment.

The allocation of investments in agriculture will be studied in three steps. The distribution of state investment will be examined first, followed by a study of the distribution of private investment. These two parts will then be integrated to provide a complete picture of the allocation pattern of total investment in the agricultural sector.

1. Distribution of State Investment in Agriculture

State investments in agriculture, water conservation, forestry, and meteorology are classified into three categories: (a) capital construction investments, mainly for the purchase of machinery and instruments and for the construction of dams and tunnels; (b) operating expenses, for establishing and maintaining various service organizations and subsidiaries for various undertakings operated by the people; and (c) working capital for various purposes. Under the First Plan, state investment for these three items totaled 8 billion yuan, of which 48.4 percent was for capital construction investment, 47.7 percent for operating expenses, and 3.9 percent for working capital.[2] Since we are concerned with fixed investment, only the first item will be dealt with in this section.

There are two series of data pertaining to the state's construction investment in agriculture--planned targets and the actual investment. Table 31 summarizes these two sets of data, both from official sources. Except for water conservation, state investment in agriculture was expressed in aggregate form without further breakdown. Of total state outlays for the agricultural sector, water conservation received the highest priority. In official literature, investment in water conservation is divided into four items. The percentage of each item in the total is as follows:[3]

Flood Control	49.4
Irrigation	20.2
Drainage	19.9
Soil conservation and other	10.5

Table 31

PLANNED AND ACTUAL STATE CAPITAL INVESTMENT
IN AGRICULTURE, 1952-1957 (IN MILLION YUAN)

	Planned		Actual	
	Total	of which water conservation	Total	of which water conservation
1952	520 [1]	331 [2]	600 [3]	410 [3]
53	588	376	770	480
54	475	219	420	220
55	556	402	620	410
56	1,262	702	1,190	710
57	983	642	1,190	730
53-57	3,864	2,341	4,190	2,550

Sources: 1. Han Pu, op. cit., p. 17
2. Communiques 1952-1953, 1956 and "The Fulfillment of the First Five Year Plan," JMJP, April 14, 1959.
3. Ten Great Years, p. 57.

But the official statistics on investment in water conservation included a great deal of underpaid work done by forced civilian labor and military workers. The drafted workers usually received only subsistence wages, far below those for other workers. The extent of underpayment, according to an estimate made by Kang Chao, roughly equals 0.20 yuan per cubic meter of construction work.[4] If we multiply the underpayment per cubic meter by the total earth work done by work-brigades, the total amount of underpayment can be roughly estimated. Adding this imputed portion to the official figure for water conservation investment, we can derive an adjusted value of investment in water conservation (Table 32).

The second major item of state agricultural investment is the reclamation of new land. There are two official statements concerning this item. One piece of information reveals that the amount of investment in reclamation of waste land by the state farms and state livestock farms under the Ministry of Agricultural Reclamation amounted to 1.1 billion yuan during the First Plan period.[5] Another official source gives a more detailed account of the total acreage reclaimed by various groups. In terms of 1,000 mou, the distribution is as follows:[6]

(1)	Total land reclaimed	47,560
(2)	Land reclaimed by agricultural cooperatives	19,800
(3)	Land reclaimed by individual migrants	6,900
(4)	Land reclaimed by state farms	20,860

The total costs of reclamation are not listed by this source. Other official sources give costs per mou ranging from 50 to 60 yuan.[7] If an average figure (55 yuan per mou) is used, the total investment in reclamation by state farms would also be about 1.1 billion yuan.

In a study of cultivated acreage and grain output, Kang Chao estimated that the investment in reclamation during the First Plan period added up to more than 1.4 billion yuan. In terms of acreage, Chao's estimate is 3.9 million mou less than the official data for state farms and individual migrant reclamation combined but is about 3 million mou larger than official figures for reclamation by state farms alone. One might infer that Chao considered half of the individual migrant reclamation as financed by state funds. Since Chao's estimates were based on annual series, which

Table 32

INVESTMENT IN WATER CONSERVATION, 1952-57, ADJUSTED

	(1) Official value of water conservation (million yuan)	(2) Total earth work done by work brigades (million m³)	(3) Under-payment of work brigades (million yuan)	(4) Adjusted investment in water conservation (million yuan)
1952	331	1,245	229	560
53	376	822	164	540
54	219	714	143	362
55	402	1,499	300	702
56	702	3,148	630	1,332
57	642	3,121	624	1,266
1953-57	2,341	9,304	1,861	4,202

Sources: Col. 1. Table 31. (The reason we used planned figures is for consistency since we used planned figures for non-agricultural sectors in Chapter 4)

Col. 2. Chao, The Construction Industry in Communist China, op. cit., p. 64.

Col. 3. Column 2 multiplied by 0.20 yuan per m³.
Col. 4. Column 1 + column 3.

presumably are more reliable, we have decided to use his estimates instead of the official aggregate data. The annual distribution of investment in land reclamation according to Chao's study was:[8]

	Area Reclaimed (million mou)	Investment (million yuan)
1952	2,808	169
53	2,330	140
54	2,539	152
55	4,450	267
56	5,521	331
57	9,013	541
53-57	23,853	1,431

The final item of state investment in agriculture involves the purchase of machinery for tractor stations and livestock for state farms, as well as costs for forestry and capital construction investment for weather bureaus and other meteorological observation facilities. When these items are added to our earlier estimates for water conservation and reclamation, total state investment in the agricultural sector can be derived (Table 33).

2. Private Investment in Agriculture

Private investment in agriculture includes projects financed by agricultural cooperatives or by peasant households. Part of the private investment can be derived from official data on producer goods sold to the rural areas. This is the portion which went through market channels and was expressed in monetary terms. The other part of private investment is the imputed value of peasants' labor in constructing water conservation projects, in reclamation of land, in improvement of soil, and in afforestation and housing repairs and construction. This part of investment did not go through the market channels and therefore was not counted as investment in official statistics. Since the effect of these labor investments is exactly the same as capital investment, the omission of this portion might result in a sizeable understatement of rural investment. We

Table 33

DISTRIBUTION OF STATE INVESTMENT IN AGRICULTURE, 1953-57
(IN MILLION YUAN)

	(1) Water Conservation		(2) Land Reclamation		(3) Purchase of Agricultural Machinery		(4) Forestry		(5) Meteorology		(6) Total
	Amount	%	Amount	%	Amount	%	Amount	%	Amount	%	Amount
1952	560	61.0	169	18.4	186	20.2	3	0.4	0		918
1953	540	56.0	140	14.5	276	28.6	7	0.7	1	0.2	964
1954	362	54.0	152	22.6	144	21.4	6	1.0	6	1.0	670
1955	702	59.4	267	22.6	199	16.8	5	0.4	7	0.8	1,180
1956	1,332	62.1	331	15.4	410	19.1	65	3.0	5	0.4	2,143
1957	1,266	55.8	541	23.8	388	17.2	63	2.8	6	0.4	2,263
53-57	4,202	58.2	1,431	19.8	1,417	19.6	149	2.0	25	0.4	7,221

Sources: Col. 1. Table 32.
Col. 2. Chao's figures given in text.
Col. 3, 4, and 5. State Statistical Bureau, Communiques for 1952, 1953, 1954, 1955, 1956 and communique on the Fulfillment of the First Five Year Plan.

have therefore decided to include it in our estimate of private investment in the rural sector.

Rural investments in capital goods have been reported in two separate sources: one gave a series of annual totals, the other reported the structure of producer goods sold to the rural areas during 1953-56. By combining these two series, we can compute the annual distribution of capital goods purchased by the rural sector.

The structure of producer goods given in Table 34 includes several items that cannot be counted as fixed investment. Fertilizer and agricultural medicine and medical implements are current expenses, building materials are included in housing construction, and implements for water conservation are included in investment in water conservation. These four items therefore must be excluded. The items which can be considered as fixed capital investments are purchases of modern and old-style farm implements and investments in livestock and carts. The annual outlays for these three items are derived in Table 35.

The portion of investment peasants provided through their own labor is difficult to measure. One official source gave an exceedingly high proportion of investment imputed to peasant investment in the following items: 93 percent of water conservation construction, 99 percent of reclamation of land, 73 percent of housing construction, and 100 percent of tree planting and afforestation. [9] According to an official survey of 228 agricultural cooperatives in 1957, total labor spent for basic construction in 1957 was 1,428,000 man-days. Since total cultivated land in these 228 cooperatives was 1,276,000 mou, for each mou, 1.1 man-days of unpaid labor was spent. [10] The same survey also revealed that of this unpaid labor, one-fourth was draft labor for the state and three-fourths was for activities within the cooperatives or within farmers' households. Since we have already imputed the drafted labor in water conservation, only the second category can be counted here. The unpaid labor of the second type was 0.82 man-days per mou. In 1957 the country possessed a cultivated area of some 1,677.5 million mou. The imputed value per man-day is set at 0.80 yuan (one official source gives 0.70 yuan). Total imputed investment in the rural area in 1957 thus amounted to 1,080 million yuan.

In view of the changing condition in collectivization and its impact on drafted labor, the above derivation is reasonable for the

Table 34

STRUCTURE OF PRODUCER GOODS PURCHASED
BY THE RURAL SECTOR, 1953-56 (IN %)

Goods	1953	1954	1955	1956	Average of 1953-56
1. Fertilizer	38.0	33.9	35.7	33.2	34.9
2. Agricultural medicines and implements	0.8	1.8	2.1	3.9	2.4
3. Modern farm implements	0.4	0.6	3.1	8.4	3.8
4. Implements for water conservation	0.0	0.5	1.0	3.7	1.6
5. Old-style farm implements	23.0	20.5	17.1	12.8	17.6
6. Building materials	0.0	7.3	11.8	11.0	8.2
7. Other producer goods*	36.7	23.4	23.3	22.8	25.8
8. Miscellaneous	1.1	12.0	5.9	4.2	5.7
9. Total	100.0	100.0	100.0	100.0	100.0

* Including livestock, carts, and producer goods for subsidary works.

Sources: Ch'u Ch'ing, Chu Chung-chien, and Wang Chih-ming, Wu-kuo Nung-tsun shih-chang ti Kai-tsu [The Reorganization of the Rural Market in Our Country] (Peking: Ts'ai-ching Chu-pan-she, 1957), p. 41.

Table 35

INVESTMENTS IN MODERN AND OLD-STYLE IMPLEMENTS
LIVESTOCK, AND CARTS, 1952-57 (IN MILLION YUAN)

	(1) Total producer goods supplied to rural areas[1]	(2) Old-style implements[2]		(3) Modern implements[2]		(4) Livestock and carts[2]	
		% of (1)	amount	% of (1)	amount	% of (1)	amount
1952	1,410	23.0	324	---	---	36.7	518
1953	1,920	23.0	442	0.4	8	36.7	704
1954	2,500	20.5	513	0.6	27	23.4	585
1955	2,820	17.1	482	3.1	116	23.3	657
1956	3,700	12.8	474	8.4	448	22.8	843
1957	3,260	12.8	418	8.4	394	22.8	743
1953-57	14,200	16.4	2,329	7.0	993	24.8	3,532

Sources: 1. Ten Great Years, p. 170.
          2. From Table 34. The 1952 figures are assumed the same as 1953; and
              the 1957 are assumed the same as 1956.

1955-57 period when collectivization was in full swing but it may be too high for the earlier years. As Kang Chao pointed out, under a collective farming system, cooperatives' authorities were inclined to use relatively more forced labor. It is assumed that the value for imputed rural investment in 1954, the year before large-scale collectivization, was about 80 percent of that in 1957, the year when China basically completed collectivization. Applying the rural population index (1957 = 100) to the two benchmark years 1954 and 1957 we can impute investment for other years roughly as shown in Table 36.

Table 36

IMPUTED RURAL LABOR INVESTMENT, 1952-57

	Rural population (1,000 persons)	Imputed investment (million yuan)
1952	503,190	835
1953	510,290	848
1954	520,170	864
1955	531,800	1,053
1956	538,650	1,066
1957	545,650	1,080
1953-57		4,911

Sources: Chao, op. cit., A-14.
The 1955 and 1956 investments are computed by applying the 1957 level and the population indexes in rural areas. The 1952 and 1953 figures are calculated by applying the 1954 level and the population indexes in rural areas.

The imputed investment thus derived is expressed in lump sums. For studying allocation, we need to disaggregate these sums into various investment items.

One major item was land reclamation. As noted previously, during the First Plan period, land reclaimed by agricultural cooperatives totaled 19,800,000 mou. If the cost of each mou is set at 50 yuan, total imputed costs must have been around 1 billion yuan.[11]

The second major item was water conservation. Data for the 228 agricultural cooperatives show that in 1957 there was a net increase in fixed assets in water conservation of 2 yuan per household, or roughly 0.4 yuan per person in the rural area. Multiplying the per capita figure by total rural population in 1957, imputed investment for water conservation in 1957 would reach 218 million yuan. Total investment in the five year period would have been around 1.1 billion yuan.

The third major item of peasant labor investment was in afforestation and tree planting. Total afforestation during 1953-57 was officially reported as 211 million mou.[12] Investment for per hectare (one hectare = 16 mou) was set at 200 yuan, or about 12.5 yuan per mou.[13] Total investment in afforestation in this period amounted to 2.6 billion yuan, of which only 149 million yuan was state investment. The rest, totaling 2.45 billion yuan, can be attributed to investment made by the peasants.

If we add these three items and subtract them from total imputed labor investment, we have a residue of 361 million yuan for investment in other areas.

By combining the imputed labor investment and the purchases in the market, we derive the total private investment in agriculture except housing presented in Table 37.

3. Allocation of Total Agricultural Investment

The complete picture of allocation of fixed capital investment in the agricultural sector becomes clearer when the state and private investments are synthesized. The result of this is shown in Table 38.

Table 38 clearly shows that fixed investment in the agricultural sector during the First Five Year Plan was concentrated in three areas: water conservation, purchases of agricultural implements,

Table 37

AMOUNT AND DISTRIBUTION OF PRIVATE FIXED INVESTMENT
IN AGRICULTURE, 1953–57

Items	Amount (million yuan)	Share %
1. Water conservation	1,100	9.3
2. Reclamation of land	1,000	8.5
3. Afforestation	2,450	20.8
4. Purchases of old-style farm implements	2,329	19.8
5. Purchases of modern implements	993	8.4
6. Purchases of livestock and carts	3,532	30.0
7. Other*	361	3.2
Total	11,765	100.0

* Mainly repairing of roads and bridges.

Sources: 1. See text.
2. Table 35.

Table 38

ALLOCATION OF TOTAL FIXED INVESTMENT IN AGRICULTURAL
SECTOR, 1953–57 (MILLION YUAN)

Items	State investment[1]	Private investment[2]	Total Amount	%
Water conservation	4,202	1,100	5,302	27.9
Reclamation	1,431	1,000	2,431	12.8
Purchases of agricultural machinery and implements[3]	709	3,322	4,031	21.2
Purchases of livestock and carts	708	3,532	4,240	22.4
Afforestation	146	2,450	2,596	13.6
Meteorology	25	0	25	0.1
Other	---	361	361	2.0
Total	7,221	11,765	18,986	100.0

Sources: 1. Table 33.
2. Table 37.
3. Includes both modern and old-typed implements.

and purchases of livestock and carts. Altogether, they constituted
more than 70 percent of the total. In terms of source of investment,
79 percent of water conservation was provided by the state. However,
in the purchases of agricultural implements and livestock and carts,
the bulk of investment came from private rather than public sources,
being 82 and 83 percent respectively.

The high priority accorded to water conservation was essentially
a continuation of Chinese tradition. From time immemorial, the
conservation and efficient use of soil and water has had special
importance in China's agricultural investment. For centuries China's
rainfall has been poorly distributed throughout the seasons. In most
localities, there was water-logging or flooding in the autumn and
drought in the spring. To remedy this situation, the Chinese Communist leaders paid great attention to water conservation. In the
early 1950s Mao said he considered irrigation "the life-blood of
agriculture. "[14] In 1951 Mao called for the harnessing of the Huai
River. During the First Plan period, great efforts were made to
control floods along the Huai and Yellow rivers. Many large
reservoirs and dams were built on principal waterways where floods
had frequently occurred. The construction of these projects made
the investment in water conservation the most important item in
Chinese fixed investment in agriculture.

Purchases of livestock and carts ranked second in agricultural
fixed investment. This represents a departure from the course of the
Soviet Union, which had an enormous decline in livestock from 1928
to 1933 because of the large-scale liquidation of livestock carried
out by individual peasants after collectivization. The share of Soviet
livestock in total agricultural capital declined substantially, from
24 percent in 1928 to merely 8 percent in 1933.[15] Although the
number of big draught animals in Mainland China increased by only
9.6 percent between 1952 and 1957, the share of livestock in total
agricultural fixed investment remains quite significant because of the
relatively small amount of capital investment in agriculture.

Purchases of agricultural machinery and implements was mainly
for the establishment of agricultural machinery and tractor stations.
By 1957 there were 390 state agricultural machinery and tractor
stations, with 12,176 tractors (in terms of 15 h.p. units), over
13,600 agricultural technical stations, and over 150 centers for pro-
moting improved farm implements.[16] In the private sector, the
bulk of investment occurred in 1956 when there was a sharp increase

in sales of new-type plows and waterwheels.

The allocation pattern of agricultural investment in China thus displayed two distinct features. First, in view of the high costs involved in new land reclamation, investment in Chinese agriculture was apparently the improvement of land already cultivated through enlargement of irrigated area and the harnessing of the major rivers. The main function was to reduce natural disasters and to achieve efficient use of soil and water. Reclamation of land occupied a much smaller share in agricultural investment than water conservation. The total area reclaimed between 1952 and 1957 was less than 2 percent of the cultivated area which indicates that the investment resources devoted to land reclamation were rather limited.

Second, since investment in agriculture was largely outside the state budget, the allocation was less deliberate. Unlike investment in industry and transportation, the distribution of investment in agriculture did not appear to have been dictated by a plan. In essence, it still followed the traditional ways, with heavy investment in labor-intensive projects like large-scale water conservation projects. This represents a departure from the Soviet model, which relies heavily on government investment in agricultural machinery.

84

FOOTNOTES

1. Ten Great Years, p. 59.

2. Han Pu, "Economize the Operating Expenses in Agriculture,"
    Chi-hua Ching-chi, No. 2, 1958, p. 17.

3. Chen Lien, "Place the Elimination of Waterlogging in an
    Important Role in Agricultural Construction," Chi-hua Ching-chi,
    No. 1, 1958, pp. 15-16.

4. Kang Chao, The Construction Industry in Communist China,
    op. cit., p. 64.

5. Ministry of Agricultural Reclamation, State Farms and Livestock
    Farms Advancing (Peking: Agriculture Publishing House, 1958),
    p. 6.

6. Chi-hua Ching-Chi, No. 2, 1958, p. 22.

7. The 50 yuan figure is derived from a statement in Chi-hua
    Ching-chi, No. 1, 1958, p. 21. The 60 yuan figure is given
    by the same publication, p. 22.

8. Chao, unpublished manuscript, op. cit., Table A 12.

9. Yueh Wei, "Principles and Methods in Studying Accumulation,"
    T'ung-chi Yen-Chiu, No. 5, 1958, pp. 16-21.

10. T'ung-chi Yen-chu, No. 8, 1958, pp. 8-12.

11. Hsiao Yu, "Reclaiming Waste Land, Enlarging the Cultivated
    Area," Chi-hua Ching-chi, No. 2, 1958, p. 22.

12. There were 16,280,000 mou in 1952, 16,690,000 mou in 1953,
    17,490,000 mou in 1954, 25,660,000 mou in 1955, 85,850,000
    mou in 1956, and 65,330,000 mou in 1957. Ten Great Years,
    p. 133.

13. The hectare figure is quoted from Chi-hua Ching-chi, No. 2,
    1958, p. 20.

14. Peking Review, No. 43 (Oct. 24, 1969), p. 17.

15. Richard Moorsteen and Raymond P. Powell, <u>The Soviet Capital Stock 1928-1962</u> (Homewood, Ill.: Richard D. Irwin, 1966), p. 158.

16. <u>Ten Great Years</u>, p. 114.

Chapter VI

SUMMARY AND CONCLUSIONS

In the preceding chapters we have discussed the allocation of fixed capital investment on both a sectoral and sub-sectoral basis during the first five years of China's industrialization. In this chapter, we want first to summarize our major findings, then to compare our findings with two other studies of Chinese capital formation, and finally to consider some implications of our findings for economic growth.

(1) Summary of Findings

The allocation pattern of fixed investment described in Chapters 3, 4, and 5 can be summarized in Table 39. In terms of the five-year average (1953-57), the largest share of investment went to industry. The share (40.6%) was very close to that of the Soviet Union during 1928-32 (41%) and was much higher than other non-Communist countries during the 1950s.

The share accorded to agriculture, taking into account both state and private investment, came out to be much higher than official statistics, which exclude private investment. The share of 22% for agricultural investment was higher than that in the Soviet Union during 1928-32 (19.1%) and also higher than non-Communist countries in 1948-58. For the other two sectors, transportation and communication and services, the share in China were invariably lower than in other countries. Only 12 percent of total fixed investment went to transportation and communication and only 8 percent was devoted to railway construction. In the Soviet First Plan, investment in railway construction occupied 13 percent, while in the initial period of U.S. industrialization (between 1880-1890), the share was as high as 21.5 percent. China's investment in all services, including housing, accounted for one-fourth of the total. This share was much lower than in other, non-Communist countries. The sectoral distribution thus demonstrates one distinct feature: a concentration of a large portion of resources in industrial development at the expense of the service sector.

Within the major economic sectors, there are two discernible trends in investment allocation. In the industrial sector, the vast bulk of fixed investment was concentrated in six branches: iron and

87

Table 39

ALLOCATION OF FIXED INVESTMENT
IN MAINLAND CHINA, 1953-57

Sector	Amount (million yuan)	Share (%)
(1) Agriculture	18,986	22.2
(A) State investment	(7,221)	(8.4)
Water conservation	4,202	4.9
Reclamation	1,431	1.6
Purchases of agricultural machinery & implements	709	0.8
Purchases of livestock and carts	708	0.8
Afforestation	146	0.2
Meteorology	25	0.1
(B) Private investment	(11,765)	(13.8)
Water conservation	1,100	1.3
Reclamation	1,000	1.2
Purchases of agricultural machinery & implements	3,322	3.8
Purchases of livestock and carts	3,532	4.2
Afforestation	2,450	2.8
Other	361	0.5
(2) Industry	34,721	40.6
Iron and steel	4,444	5.2
Building materials	591	0.7
Chemicals Non-ferrous metals	4,826	5.6
Coals	4,479	5.2
Petroleum	1,076	1.3

Table 39 (continued)

Sector	Amount (million yuan)	Share (%)
(2) Industry (continued)		
Electric power	4,028	4.7
Metal-processing	5,173	6.1
Defense industry	5,312	6.2
Textiles	1,875	2.2
Food processing	764	0.9
Paper-making	591	0.7
Other	1,562	1.8
(3) Transportation and Communication	10,413	12.2
Railways	6,856	8.0
Other	3,557	4.2
(4) Dwellings	11,476	13.4
State investment	3,626	4.2
Private investment	7,850	9.2
(5) Other	9,899	11.6
Total Fixed investment	85,495	100.0

steel, chemicals, non-ferrous metals, coal, electric power, and metal-processing. Altogether, they accounted for more than 80 percent of the total, while investment in consumer good industries accounted for only 12 percent of fixed industrial investment. This was a striking departure from investment policy in the pre-Communist era, when consumer goods, particularly the textile industry, received the largest share of investment.

In contrast, investment within the agricultural sector still by and large followed traditional patterns. The main effort was concentrated in labor-intensive projects such as water conservation and afforestation rather than in pushing mechanization of agriculture.

(2) Comparison with Other Studies

As we have noted, this study is not the first attempt at an independent appraisal of China's fixed capital formation. Two major efforts to estimate Chinese capital formation during the First Plan period have been conducted by K.C. Yeh and by William Hollister. Although their main focus was on the aggregate level, both did provide discussions of sectoral allocation. The existence of these previous estimates invites a comparison with those of the current study.

K.C. Yeh's estimate of capital formation basically used official investment data with adjustments to achieve conceptual consistency. The aggregate investment computed by him included four major components: (a) state investment, (b) non-state farm investment, (c) non-state non-farm investment, and (d) major repairs. Items (a) and (d) were taken primarily from official statistics, while items (b) and (c) were derived by the commodity flow method. Since Yeh used estimating procedures not completely identical with ours, some differences in the findings are inevitable.

Hollister's estimates for fixed capital investment were derived as the sum of agricultural investment, non-agricultural state investment, and other non-agricultural investment. While the procedures used in his revised estimates are not known, his original procedure included two major steps: First, he estimated agricultural investment by (a) estimating total agriculture investment for 1952 from some sample data, (b) dividing this total into extra-sectoral investment purchases and intra-sectoral purchases, and (c) extending the two estimates for 1952 to cover the entire period by using an index. Second, he derived state investment by summing budget expenditures for capital construction less 3.2 percent for cash reserves plus major repairs expenditures and miscellaneous gross investment budget expenditures for agriculture, water conservation and forestry.[1]

The defects of Hollister's estimation procedures have been critically reviewed by K.C. Yeh[2] and require no further elaboration here. Hollister's revised estimates published in 1966 are the ones we will use for comparison here.

If we compare the allocation patterns depicted by Yeh and Hollister with our estimates, both similarities and differences can be discerned. As shown in Table 40, the share of investment allocated to the agricultural sector is higher in our estimate than in Yeh's. Since Hollister's estimate of agricultural investment includes housing, the exclusion of housing investment would also put his estimated share in agriculture below ours.

For investment in industry, our estimate fell between the two poles of Yeh's and Hollister's, being 6 percentage points lower than Yeh's and 3 percentage points higher than Hollister's. Yeh's estimated share for transportation and communications also is invariably higher than Hollister's and ours. Consequently, investment going to the M+ sector as estimated by Yeh was 8.5 percentage points higher than ours and 12 percentage points higher than Hollister's.

For the share of investment going to services, our estimates are also mid-way between Yeh's and Hollister's, being 6 percentage points higher than Yeh's, and 4 percentage points lower than Hollister's. Although such a comparison can neither confirm nor deny the validity of any of these three measurements, it does serve to indicate that our estimate is the least extreme one.

Despite marked differences among specific aspects of these three estimates, the fundamental findings concerning the pattern of allocation of fixed investment during Communist China's First Five-Year Plan are quite similar. Throughout the period, industry's share was consistently higher than that of the other sectors. The share of agriculture averaged from 20 to 24 percent of the total fixed investment, considerably lower than that for industry. Of all four sectors, the smallest share of investment went to transportation and communications, and it showed no discernible upward or downward trend. Investment in the remaining sectors accounted for from one-fifth to one-third of total investment, and this share declined continuously after 1953. A major conclusion shared by these three estimates is that the great expansion in productive capacity during the First Plan was achieved at the expense of investment in social over-

Table 40

COMPARISON OF THREE ESTIMATES OF ALLOCATION OF FIXED INVESTMENT, 1952-57

	(1) Agriculture			(2) Industry			(3) Transportation and Communication			(4) M+ Sector (2+3)			(5) Services			(6) Total (1)+(4)+(5)
	Cheng	Yeh	Hol.	Cheng	Yeh	Hol.	Cheng	Yeh	Hol.	Cheng	Yeh	Hol.	Cheng	Yeh	Hol.	
1952	31.4	32.0	24.9	29.1	35.5	28.7	11.2	13.5	10.3	40.3	49.0	39.0	28.3	19.0	36.2	100
1953	25.4	21.1	20.7	33.9	39.2	33.0	10.0	12.0	9.4	43.9	51.2	42.4	30.5	27.7	36.7	100
1954	18.8	16.7	22.4	39.5	44.5	34.4	12.4	14.5	11.0	51.9	59.0	45.4	29.2	24.2	32.3	100
1955	22.2	19.2	24.5	40.4	46.1	34.3	13.9	16.4	13.8	54.3	62.5	48.1	23.4	18.2	27.3	100
1956	21.6	18.8	22.8	40.4	47.2	37.8	12.8	15.9	13.8	53.2	63.1	51.6	25.2	18.2	25.4	100
1957	23.2	17.8	23.0	45.4	52.1	41.3	11.3	13.8	12.6	56.7	65.9	53.9	20.1	16.3	23.1	100
1952-57	23.8	20.9	23.1	38.1	44.1	34.9	11.9	14.4	11.8	50.0	58.5	46.7	26.2	20.6	30.2	100

Sources: Cheng: From Table 13, Chapter III.
Yeh: "Capital Formation" in Eckstein, Galenson & Liu, eds., Economic Trends in Communist China, p. 521.
Hollister: "Trends in Capital Formation in Communist China," in Joint Economic Committee, U.S. Congress, An Economic Profile of Mainland China, p. 128.

head capital: housing, transportation, and urban facilities. Many facets of agriculture and light industry were also greaty neglected.

(3) Implications for Economic Growth

In essence, the allocation of investments among the various economic sectors in the initial phase of China's industrialization was quite consistent with the established goals of the Communist central authorities, namely to achieve a high rate of growth and a high degree of self-sufficiency in capital goods.

First, industrialization involves a continuous transformation of the economic structure, most particularly a shift from agriculture to industry. The structural transformation of the traditional sector seems to be a necessary condition for cumulative and self-sustaining growth. A distinctive feature of the Chinese economy is the predominance of an agricultural sector characterized by widespread disguised unemployment and high rates of population growth. In such a setting, the heart of the development problem lies in the gradual shift of the economy's center of gravity from the agricultural to the industrial sector. The growth of industry requires a high rate of capital investment to expand its facilities and to adopt modern technology. In the 33 years of industrialization in the Soviet Union (from 1928 to 1961), the increase in capital appears to have accounted for roughly a fifth to a half or more of the total growth in output. The contribution of capital becomes even greater when the dependence of technological change upon capital is taken into account. [3] In this sense, the allocation of a large proportion of fixed investment to industry must be considered a requisite for rapid growth.

Second, empirical data for other developed countries illustrate that there are wide variations among different sectors of an economy in the demands they make on capital. The capital/output ratio in manufacturing is usually relatively low, while the ratios in agriculture, transportation, and public utilities are often extremely high. For instance, the capital/output (fixed capital) ratio in the USA in 1933 was 1.35 for agriculture and 2.55 for transportation and communications, but only 0.38 for primary manufacturing and 0.55 for secondary manufacturing. [4] In the case of the Soviet Union, the average capital/output ratio (net capital stock/gross national product) during 1928-40 in the non-agricultural, non-residential sector ranged from 1.12 to 1.79, while the ratio for the entire economy ranged from 1.71 to 1.93. [5] If manufacturing is able to make some headway before investment in agriculture and social overheads become heavy, the rate of growth for the economy would be higher than if the scarce capital were spread among all sectors.

Third, development experiences in other countries suggest the need to discriminate between the use of scarce and relatively abundant resources. Investible funds are in short supply, and labor continues to be an abundant factor. Under these conditions, the development of agriculture has to rely more on labor-intensive techniques in order to save capital for industry.

For all these reasons, one would be inclined to defend rather than reject the Chinese decision in the First Plan to concentrate more investible funds in industry. The defect of Chinese investment policy stems instead from three other problems.

First, Chinese industrial expansion during the First Plan period seems to have been solely for the purpose of continuous expansion of producer goods industries and the defense industries, with very little linkage to agriculture or to the traditional sectors. The chemical fertilizers industry in the 1952-57 period was merely nominal, and modern tractor production was not started until 1958. Without a feedback from the industrial sector, the source of agriculture's support to industrial development was soon exhausted. Despite all signs of take-off during the First Five-Year Plan, the Chinese economy did not escape the "low-level equilibrium trap," as R. Nelson called it.[6] In the following ten years, the Chinese economy went through a cycle of upsurge (1958-60), recession (1961-63), and recovery (1964-66), with a very low rate of growth for the period as a whole. Apparently, the "big push" in the modern sector did not push the entire economy into sustained growth.

Apart from the lack of linkage between industry and agriculture, China's development policy also neglected the problem of employment. More than 85 percent of capital investment in industry during the First Plan period was concentrated in the 694 large industrial projects, which are capital-intensive, have a long period of gestation, and have a low employment-generating effect. Between 1952 and 1957, employment in the industrial sector increased by 1.78 million, which accounted for only 9 percent of the additions to the labor force (estimated at an annual rate of 4 million in that period). Moreover, the increase in employment in modern industry was partially offset by the decline of employment in traditional sectors (mainly handicrafts). Consequently, the growth of non-agricultural employment was very moderate (Table 41). In this situation, the rural proportion of the population was not materially reduced, being 86.8 percent in 1953 and 85.7 percent in 1957.[7]

Table 41

CHANGES IN EMPLOYMENT IN NONAGRICULTURAL
SECTORS, 1952-57 (%)

Year	Modern Sector	Traditional Sector	Total Change
1952	+ 23.2	- 3.4	+ 4.7
1953	+ 15.4	+ 0.5	+ 5.6
1954	+ 2.9	- 3.9	- 1.3
1955	+ 1.5	- 6.2	- 3.0
1956	+ 26.9	- 10.5	+ 4.8
1957	- 0.1	+ 1.6	+ 0.2

Source: C. M. Hou, "Manpower, Employment, and Unemployment" in Economic Trends in Communist China, op. cit., p. 361.

This would suggest that despite the sharp increase of capital investment in the modern sector, the distribution of population between urban and rural areas remains roughly unchanged. As the economy's center of gravity stayed with agriculture, this source of savings cannot be sustained or expanded without increases in agricultural productivity.

The third problem lies in agricultural investment policy. As noted previously, Chinese investment in the agricultural sector was focused on labor-intensive projects, particularly water conservation. Most of the irrigation projects were conducted by mobilizing mass participation of peasants without necessary geological surveys and engineering designs. The central authorities seemed to feel that the application of modern science and technology was not so significant for agriculture as for industry. Little attempt was made to introduce new technology to rural areas. Large-scale agricultural research was not started until March 1957, when the Academy of Agricultural Science was first established as the leading national center for agricultural research. [8] Application of chemical fertilizers was trivial, and activities that facilitated wide use of the most productive plant varieties and of improved farm practices were hardly

begun. Because the large share of investment went to water conservation and most of the irrigation projects proved to be ineffective--
and in many cases even harmful--the fixed investment in the agricultural sector thus contributed very little to agricultural productivity.
In fact, there was a positive correlation between the scale of water
conservation work and the increase of disaster-affected areas. Before
the grand-scale water conservation work of 1956, the disaster areas
in China never exceeded 30 million acres. After the 1956 mass water
conservation projects, the areas suffering from flood and drought increased, from 18 million acres in 1955 to 38 million acres in 1957,
78 million acres in 1958, 108 million acres in 1959, and 150 million
acres in 1960.[9] This would suggest that the ill-planned large-scale
irrigation works brought about negative rather than positive effects
for agricultural production.

The combined effect of the lack of linkage between industry
and agriculture, the concentration of industrial investments in capital-
intensive projects, and the inefficiency of investment in the agricultural sector caused a low rate of growth in urban employment, an
increase in disguised underemployment in the rural areas, and a
decline in agricultural productivity.[10] The decline of agricultural
productivity forestalls further expansion of the industrial sector.
This might explain why China's economy, after remarkable progress
in the First Plan period, came to a standstill in the period following.

The Chinese experiences support several general conclusions
relating to the allocation of capital investment:

(1)   The effect of capital investment on economic growth de-
        pends not merely on the rate of investment but more
        significantly on how the capital is allocated. During the
        Chinese First Plan, the rate of investment was as high
        as 21 percent, far exceeding the minimum requirement
        for take-off as set by Rostow. However the Chinese
        economy failed to achieve a sustained growth afterward,
        indicating that mistakes in allocation policy might have
        been responsible for a part of the failure.

(2)   In a predominantly agrarian economy, a rapid expansion
        of the industrial sector is the key to escape the "low-
        level equilibrium trap." However if the trap is to be
        avoided, the expanding industrial sector must be able to
        absorb a large amount of surplus labor from agriculture

and to render a significant contribution to the rise of agricultural productivity. This would require the allocation of the bulk of industrial capital to labor-intensive projects and to those heavy industries linked to the rise of agricultural productivity.

(3) In a country like China, where the capacity of the agricultural sector to support industrialization is rather limited, there are competing claims on the scarce resources needed by both agricultural and industrial development. The change of priorities from the "heavy industry first" of the First Five-Year Plan period, to "agriculture first" after 1961 clearly reflected the small tolerance of traditional agriculture for being squeezed in support of industry.

(4) In the short run, inadequacy of investment in transportation may be compensated for by the existence of a large labor force in the traditional transportation sector, and by squeezing the maximum of service from the inherited tracks and rolling stock. But this resource is rapidly exhausted. The debt to the future will soon fall due. In the case of housing and urban facilities, rising demand is inevitable, since industrialization always entails rapid urbanization, which in turn requires continuous expansion in housing and urban facilities.

All these factors seem to point to the final conclusion that in the course of industrialization it is plausible to concentrate investment funds in one particular sector in order to achieve a high rate of growth in the short run. However, no unbalanced development strategy can be effective for long if it does not pay greater attention to the hitherto neglected sectors.

FOOTNOTES

1. W. Hollister, China's Gross National Product and Social Accounts 1950-1957, op. cit., p. 59.

2. See K.C. Yeh, "Capital Formation in Mainland China: 1931-36 and 1952-57" (unpublished dissertation), 1965, pp. 125-130.

3. Moorstein and Powell, The Soviet Capital Stock 1928-1962, op. cit., pp. 305-306.

4. A.K. Cairncross, "Capital Formation in the Take-off," in Rostow, ed., The Economics of Take-Off Into Sustained Growth, op. cit., p. 256.

5. Moorstein and Powell, op. cit., p. 367, Table T-53.

6. R.R. Nelson, "The Low Level Equilibrium Trap in Underdeveloped Economies," American Economic Review, Dec. 1956.

7. The 1953 figure is from "China's Population 1949-56," TCKT, No. 11, June 14, 1957; the 1957 figure is from Wang Kuangwei, "Views on Allocating Agricultural Labor," CHCC, No. 8, 1957, pp. 6-9.

8. Chu-yuan Cheng, Scientific and Engineering Manpower In Communist China, op. cit., pp. 26-27.

9. Chu-yuan Cheng, Communist China's Economy 1949-62, South Orange, N.J., Seton Hall University Press, 1963, pp. 143-44.

10. According to Anthony Tang, agricultural productivity in 1957 was only 94.4 percent of that in 1952. See Anthony M. Tang, "Policy and Performance in Agriculture," in Economic Trends in Communist China, op. cit., p. 489.

APPENDICES

Appendix 1

ESTIMATION OF GROSS FIXED INVESTMENT IN FARMS, 1952–57
(MILLION YUAN)

	1952	1953	1954	1955	1956	1957
Rural housing construction[1]	1,180	820	1,240	1,420	2,660	1,710
Modern farm implements[2]	0	8	27	116	448	394
Old-type implements[2]	324	442	513	482	474	418
Livestock and carts[2]	518	704	585	657	843	743
Water conservation[3]	560	540	362	702	1,332	1,266
Reclamation[3]	169	140	152	267	331	541
Other imputed investment[4]	835	848	864	1,053	1,066	1,080
State investment in agriculture, forestry, and meteorology	189	284	156	210	480	460
Total	3,775	3,786	3,899	4,907	7,634	6,612

Sources and notes: 1. Table 6, Chapter 2.
2. Table 35, Chapter 5.
3. Table 33, Chapter 5.
4. Table 36, Chapter 5.
5. From State Statistical Bureau, Communiques for 1952, 1953, 1954, 1955, 1956 and the Fulfillment of the First Five-Year Plan.

Appendix 2

ALLOCATION OF GROSS FIXED INVESTMENT BY ECONOMIC SECTOR, 1952-57

Figures in Table 13, Chapter 3 were derived by the following steps:
(1) From official statistics in Ten Great Years, pp. 59-60, we know the percentage distribution of capital construction investment among various sectors as follows:

Table A.1

	Total	Indus- try	Build- ing	Prospect- ing for resources	Agri- cul- ture	Trans- porta- tion & commu- nica- tions	Trade	Culture & sci- entific research	Public health & wel- fare	Urban public utili- ties	Govern- ment bureaus	Other
1952	100	38.8	2.1	1.6	13.8	17.5	2.8	6.4	1.3	3.9	0.4	11.4
1953	100	35.4	4.5	2.4	9.7	13.4	3.4	7.8	1.9	3.1	3.4	15.0
1954	100	42.3	3.9	3.2	4.6	16.5	4.3	7.5	1.7	2.6	2.3	11.1
1955	100	46.2	3.5	2.7	6.7	19.0	3.7	6.3	1.1	2.4	1.5	6.9
1956	100	46.1	4.4	2.7	8.0	17.7	5.1	6.7	0.7	2.4	1.1	5.1
1957	100	52.3	3.3	2.2	8.6	15.0	2.7	6.7	0.9	2.8	1.3	4.2
1953-57	100	45.5	3.9	2.6	7.6	16.4	3.9	6.9	1.2	2.6	1.8	11.4

Appendix 2 (continued)

(2) Deducting agricultural investment from the total in Table A.1, we can derive non-agricultural investment. The percentage distribution of the non-agricultural investment is calculated as follows:

Table A.2

	Total	Indus-try	Build-ing	Prospect-ing for resources	Transporta-tion & communications	Trade	Culture & scien-tific research	Public health & wel-fare	Urban public utili-ties	Govern-ment bureaus	Other
1953	100	39.2	5.0	2.7	14.8	3.8	8.6	2.1	3.4	3.8	16.6
1954	100	44.3	4.1	3.4	17.2	4.5	7.8	1.8	2.8	2.5	11.6
1955	100	49.5	3.8	2.9	20.2	4.0	6.8	1.2	2.6	1.6	7.4
1956	100	50.1	4.8	2.9	19.2	5.5	7.3	0.8	2.6	1.2	5.6
1957	100	57.2	3.6	2.4	16.4	3.0	7.3	1.0	3.1	1.4	4.6

Appendix 2 (continued)

(3) Multiplying the percentages in Table A.2 by the aggregate figures for non-agricultural sectors in Table 10, Chapter 2, the investment in each of the non-agricultural sectors is calculated as follows:

Table A.3
(in million yuan)

	Total	Indus-try	Build-ing	Prospect-ing for resources	Transporta-tion & com-munications	Trade	Culture & scien-tific research	Public health & wel-fare	Urban public utili-ties	Govern-ment bureaus	Other
1953	7,906	3,099	395	213	1,170	301	680	166	269	301	1,312
1954	10,180	4,510	417	346	1,751	458	769	183	285	255	1,181
1955	10,770	5,332	409	312	2,176	431	732	129	280	172	797
1956	15,356	7,693	738	446	2,948	844	1,121	123	399	185	859
1957	14,445	8,263	521	346	2,368	433	1,054	144	448	203	665

Appendix 2 (continued)

(4) Adding investment in the agricultural sector to Table A.3, distribution of both agricultural and non-agricultural sectors can be derived. The percentages are then regrouped into five broad sectors:

1. Agriculture - including both state and private investments but excluding rural housing investments, which are added to urban housing investment to form an independent sector.

2. Industry - including manufacturing, building, prospecting for natural resources, and urban utilities.

3. Transportation and communications - including railways, highways, other modern means of transportation, postal service, and telecommunications.

4. Dwellings - including urban and rural housing construction.

5. Other services - including public administration, trade, culture, public health and welfare.

Appendix 3

SECTORAL INCREMENTAL CAPITAL/OUTPUT RATIO

Sector	Incremental Output (1952-57) (million yuan)		Cumulated gross fixed investment[2] (1952-56) (million yuan)	Cumulated net fixed investment[3] (1952-56) (million yuan)	ICOR	
	GNP[1]	NNP[1]			Gross	Net
Whole economy	26,150	23,930	72,690	52,270	2.8	2.2
Agriculture	3,970	2,970	16,680	7,510	4.2	2.5
Industry	15,460	14,990	27,550	23,200	1.8	1.5
Transportation and communications	1,790	1,500	8,950	6,160	5.0	4.1
Other	4,930	4,470	19,510	15,400	3.9	3.4

Sources and notes: 1. Incremental output for 1952-57 is the value-added figures given in Liu and Yeh, The Economy of the Chinese Mainland, p. 66. Figures for the whole economy are directly quoted from Liu and Yeh's study. The sectoral breakdowns in that study are expressed in NNP. The GNP figures are derived by the following steps:

(a) Net output for each sector from Liu-Yeh's Table 8 is adjusted to fit our sectoral classification. The industry sector consists of factories, handicrafts, mining, utilities, and construction. The "other sectors" include trade, government administration, finance, personal services, residential rents, and work brigades.

Appendix 3 (continued)

Sources and notes:

(b) The incremental depreciation between 1952 and 1957 (2.22 billion yuan), calculated from Liu-Yeh Table 8, is distributed among the four sectors by the following weights: 45% for agriculture, 21% for industry, 13% for transportation and communications, and 21% for other sectors. These weights are based on the distribution of depreciation for these sectors during 1952-56.

(c) The incremental depreciation charges are then added to the incremental net output for the four sectors to derive sectoral incremental gross output.

2. Cumulated gross fixed investments are from Table 14.

3. The net investments are calculated by the following procedures:

(a) For the economy as a whole, the net investment is derived by deducting depreciation for 1952-56--totaling 20.42 billion yuan as estimated by Liu-Yeh--from gross investment.

(b) For industry, Ishikawa estimated that the total depreciation charge including major repairs in the public sector in 1953-56 was 7.31 billion yuan (Ishikawa, op. cit., Tables 11-12, p. 147). The 1952 depreciation is estimated at 70% of 1953. Total depreciation for 1952-56 for the public sector amounted to 8.21 billion yuan. Since the share of industrial fixed assets in the total

Appendix 3 (continued)

Sources and notes:

value of non-farm fixed assets was 50% in 1952 and 56% in 1955 (Ishikawa, op. cit., p. 109), if we assume a mean value of these two figures (53%) for the 1952-56 period, depreciation charges for the industrial sector during this period would be 8.21 x 0.53 = 4.35 billion yuan.

(c) For transportation and communications, the percentage in 1955 was 33% of the non-farm fixed asset (Ishikawa, op. cit., p. 109). The average share for the 1952-56 period was about 34%. Depreciation charges for this sector can then be derived as 2.79 billion yuan (8.21 x 0.34 = 2.79).

(d) No official information for depreciation in the agricultural sector was found. The depreciation rate for the whole economy is calculated at 20.42 ÷ 72.69 = 28% and depreciation for the non-farm sectors is calculated as 8,210 ÷ 56,012 = 14.6%. Since the weights between agriculture and non-agricultural sectors in the fixed investment are calculated as 33 and 67 (Table 2), the depreciation for the agricultural sector can be derived from the following equations:

$$0.28 = (0.67 \times 14.6\%) + 0.33X$$

$$X = \frac{0.28 - (0.146 \times 0.67)}{0.33}$$

$$= 55\%$$

Appendix 3 (continued)

Sources and notes: (e)   Depreciation for other sectors is derived as a residual:

$$20.42 - (9.17 + 4.35 + 2.79) = 4.11$$

BIBLIOGRAPHY

(1) Primary Sources

Chai Mao-chou. "Our Method of Forecasting the Implementation of Investment Plans." T'ung-chi Kung-tso [Statistical Work]. Peking, No. 4, 1957.

Chang Cheng. "Improve and Apply the Method of Computing Completed Investment." T'ung-chi Kung-tso T'ung hsün [Statistical Work Bulletin]. Peking, No. 7, 1956.

Ch'ang Sheng and Wang En-jung. "A Brief Discussion on Fixed Assets and Depreciation in the Industrial Enterprises." Ching-chi Yen-chiu [Economic Research]. Peking, No. 5, 1956.

Chang Wei-ta. "On the Method of Computing Indicators of Depreciation of Productive Fixed Assets." Ching-chi Yen-chiu. No. 3, 1956.

Chao I-wen. Hsin-chung-kuo ti Kung-yeh [Industry in New China]. Peking: T'ung-chi Chu-pan-she, 1957.

Chen Lien. "Place the Elimination of Waterlogging in An Important Role in Agricultural Construction." Chi-hua Ching-chi [Planned Economy]. Peking, No. 1, 1958.

Chinese Academy of Sciences, Economic Research Section, Handicraft Group. 1954-nien Ch'uan-kuo Ko-t'i Shou-kung-yeh Tiao-ch'a Tzu-liao [Data of the 1954 National-wide Handicraft Investigation]. Peking: San-lien-su-tien, 1957.

Chu Ch'eng-p'ing. "Discussion of Some Problems Concerning the National Income." Ching-chi Yen-chiu. No. 3, 1957.

Ch'u Ch'ing, Chu Chung-chien and Wang Chih-ming. Wu-kuo Nung-tsun Shih-chang Ti Kai-tsu [The Reorganization of the Rural Markets in Our Country]. Peking: Ts'ai-cheng Chu-pan-she, 1957.

Ch'u Ching-hui. "An Explanation of the Major Changes in the Tabulation Forms for the National Economic Plan." Chi-hua Ching-chi. No. 8, 1957.

Fan Wei-chung. Ti-i-ko Wu-nien Chi-hua Chieh-sho [Explanation of the First Five-year Plan]. Peking: Kung-jen Chu-pan-she, 1955.

First Five-year Plan for Development of the National Economy of the People's Republic of China, 1953-1957. Peking: Foreign Languages Press, 1956.

Fu Shih-hsin. "The Role of the Handicraft Industry in the National Economy." Ta-kung-pao. Peking: July 1, 1959.

Han Pu. "Economize the Operating Expenses in Agriculture." Chi-hua Ching-chi. No. 2, 1958.

Hsiao Yu. "Reclaiming Waste Land, Enlarging the Cultivated Area." Chi-hua Ching-chi. No. 2, 1958.

Hsieh Mu-ch'iao. "How to Strengthen and Improve Basic Construction Work." T'ung-chi Kung-tso T'ung-hsün. No. 6, 1956.

Hsu Chien, Tsi Shih-kuang, and Yu Tao. Ching-chi T'ung-chi-hsüeh Chiang-hua [Lectures on Economic Statistics]. Peking: T'ung-chi Chu-pan-she, 1957.

Huang Min-hsin. "The Problems of Calculating Peasants' Accumulation." T'ung-chi Kung-tso. No. 19, 1957.

Liu Kuo-kuang and Liang Wen-sen. "A Note on the Relationship between the Compensation of Moral Obsolescence of Fixed Assets and Their Depreciation." Ching-chi Yen-chiu. No. 9, 1963.

Ma Yin-chu. Wo-ti Ching-chi-li-lun Che-hsüeh-si-hsiang ho Cheng-chih-li-chang [My Economic Theory, Philosophy and Political Stand]. Peking: Ts'ai-cheng Chu-pan-she, 1958.

Ministry of Agricultural Reclamation. State Farms and Livestock Farms Advancing. Peking: Agricultural Publishing House, 1958.

Niu Chung-huang. Wo-kuo Kuo-min Shou-ju ti Chi-lei ho Hsiao-fei [Accumulation and Consumption in China's National Income]. Peking: Chung-kuo Ch'ing-nien Chu-pan-she, 1957.

State Statistical Bureau. "A General Survey of National Industrial Capital." T'ung-chi Kung-tso. No. 1, 1957.

State Statistical Bureau. "Several Major Problems Concerning the Computation of Completed Investment in Basic Construction." T'ung-chi Kung-tso. No. 10, 1957.

State Statistical Bureau. "A General Survey of China's Socialist Industrialization." Hsin-hua Pan-yueh-kan [New China Semi-monthly]. Peking, No. 2, 1957.

State Statistical Bureau. "Great Achievements in China's Basic Construction in the Past Seven Years." T'ung-chi Kung-tso. No. 17, 1957.

State Statistical Bureau. "On the Fulfillment of the 1956 State Economic Plan." Jen-ming Jih-pao [People's Daily]. September 15, 1957.

State Statistical Bureau. "On the Fulfillment of the First Five-year Plan." Jen-ming Jih-pao. April 14, 1959.

State Statistical Bureau. Ten Great Years, Statistics of the Economic and Cultural Achievements of the People's Republic of China. Peking: Foreign Languages Press, 1960.

State Statistical Bureau. Wo-kuo Kang-tieh, Tien-li, Mei-t'an, Chi-hsieh, Fang-chih, Tsao-chih Kung-yeh ti Chin-hsi. [The Present and Past of China's Iron and Steel, Electrical Power, Coal, Machinery, Textile and Paper Industries]. Peking: T'ung-chi Chu-pan-she, 1958.

State Statistical Bureau, Research Office. "A Preliminary Study of the Production and Distribution of Our National Income." T'ung-chi Yen-chiu [Statistical Research]. Peking: January, 1958.

Sun Yeh-fang. "Discussion on Gross Output Value and Other Topics." T'ung-chi Kung-tso. No. 13, 1957.

T'ung-chi Kung-tso. "China's Population, 1949-1956.", No. 11, 1957.

T'ung-chi Kung-tso T'ung-hsün. "Basic Situation of Construction Industry in Our Country." No. 24, 1956.

T'ung-chi Yen-chiu. "Data from the Typical Survey of the Distribution of Income in 228 Agricultural Producers' Cooperatives in 1957." No. 8, 1958.

112

Wang Kuang-wei. "Some Views on Allocating Agricultural Labor."
Chi-hua Ching-chi. No. 8, 1957.

Wang Kuang-wei. "Strengthen Industry's Aid to Agriculture." Hung-
ch'i [Red Flag]. No. 16, 1959.

Wang Tieh-sheng. "To Understand Better the Relationship between
Light Industry and Capital Accumulation." Hsüeh-hsi [Study].
No. 6, March 18, 1957.

Yang Po. "The Relationship between Accumulation and Consumption
in the National Income of our Country." Hsin-hua Pan-yueh-kan.
No. 22, 1958.

Yang Ying-chieh. A Report on A Survey of Five Agricultural Cooperatives and 600 Peasant Households. Peking: Ts'ai-cheng Ching-
chi Chu-pan-she, 1958.

Yueh Wei. "The Method of Computing National Income." Ching-chi
Yen-chiu. No. 3, 1956.

Yueh Wei. "Principles and Methods in Studying Accumulation." T'ung-
chi Yen-chiu. No. 5, 1958.

Yueh Wei. "On the Problems of Accumulation by Agricultural Producers' Cooperatives." Hsüeh-hsi. No. 7, 1958.

(2)   Secondary Sources

Bain, Joe S.   International Differences in Industrial Structure.   New Haven: Yale University Press, 1966.

Bhatt, V. V.   "Capital-Output Ratios of Certain Industries: A Comparative Study of Certain Countries."   The Review of Economics and Statistics.   August, 1954.

Bhatt, V. V.   "Savings and Capital Formation."   Economic Development and Cultural Change.   Vol. VII, No. 3, 1959.

Cairncross, A. K.   "Capital Formation in the Take-Off."   The Economics of Take-Off into Sustained Growth.   Edited by Rostow. New York: St. Martin's Press, 1965.

Chao, Kang.   "Fixed Capital Investment in Communist China."   (Unpublished manuscript).   Center for Chinese Studies, The University of Michigan, 1968.

Chao, Kang.   The Construction Industry in Communist China. Chicago: Aldine, 1968.

Chen, Nai-Ruenn.   Chinese Economic Statistics, A Handbook for Mainland China.   Chicago: Aldine, 1967.

Cheng, Chu-yuan.   Communist China's Economy 1949-1962, Structual Changes and Crisis.   New Jersey: Seton Hall University Press 1963.

Cheng, Chu-yuan.   Scientific and Engineering Manpower in Communist China.   Washington D. C.: National Science Foundation, 1966.

Cheng, Chu-yuan.   The Machine-Building Industry in Communist China.   Chicago: Aldine-Atherton, 1971.

Cheng, Chu-yuan.   The Economy of Communist China 1949-1969. Ann Arbor: University of Michigan, Center for Chinese Studies, 1971.

Eckstein, Alexander.   The National Income of Communist China. New York: Free Press of Glencoe, 1961.

Galenson, Walter and Harvey Leibenstein. "Investment Criteria, Productivity and Economic Development." Quarterly Journal of Economics. August, 1955.

Hirschman, Albert. The Strategy of Economic Development. New Haven: Yale University Press, 1958.

Hollister, W. William. China's Gross National Product and Social Accounts, 1950-1957. New York: Free Press of Glencoe, 1958.

Hollister, W. William. "Trends in Capital Formation in Communist China." An Economic Profile of Mainland China. U.S. Congress, Joint Economic Committee. 1967.

Hou, Chih-ming. "Manpower, Employment and Unemployment." Economic Trends Communist China. Edited by Eckstein, Galenson and Liu. Chicago: Aldine, 1968.

Ishikawa, Shigeru. National Income and Capital Formation in Mainland China: An Examination of Official Statistics. Tokyo: Institute of Asian Economic Affairs, 1965.

Kaplan, Norman. "Capital Formation and Allocation." Soviet Economic Growth, Conditions and Perspective. Edited by Abram Bergson. Evanston, Illinois: Row, Peterson, 1953.

Kaplan, Norman. "Capital Stock." Economic Trends in the Soviet Union. Edited by Bergson and Kuznets. Cambridge: Harvard University Press, 1963.

Kuznets, Simon. "Capital Formation Proportions." Economic Development and Cultural Change. Vol. 8, No. 4, Part II, July, 1960.

Kuznets, Simon. "Quantitative Aspects of the Economic Growth of Nations, VI: Long-Term Trends in Capital Formations." Economic Development and Cultural Change. Vol. IX, No. 4, Part II, July, 1961.

Li, Choh-ming, ed. Industrial Development In Communist China, New York: Praeger, 1964.

Li, Choh-ming. Economic Development of Communist China. Berkeley and Los Angeles: University of California Press, 1959.

Li, Choh-ming. The Statistical System of Communist China. Berkeley and Los Angeles: University of California Press, 1962.

Liu, Ta-chung and Yeh Kung-chia. The Economy of Chinese Mainland, National Income and Economic Development, 1933-1959. Princeton, New Jersey: Princeton University Press, 1965.

Moorsteen, Richard and Raymond Powell, The Soviet Capital Stock 1928-1962. Homewood, Illinois: Richard D. Irwin, 1968.

Nelson, R. R. "The Low Level Equilibrium Trap in Underdeveloped Economies." American Economic Review. Dec., 1956.

Nurkse, Ragnar. Problems of Capital Formation in Underdeveloped Countries and Patterns of Trade and Development. New York: Oxford University Press, 1967.

Rostow, W. W., ed. The Economics of Take-Off into Sustained Growth. New York: St. Martin's Press, 1965.

Shinohara, Miyokei. "Capital Formation in Post-War Japan, A Statistical Evaluation." Asian Studies in Income and Wealth. Bombay, India: Asia Publishing House, 1965.

Tang, Anthony. "Policy and Performance in Agriculture." Economic Trends in Communist China. Edited by Eckstein, Galenson and Liu. Chicago: Aldine, 1968.

Yeh, Kung-chia. "Capital Formation in Mainland China, 1931-36, and 1952-57." (Unpublished Dissertation, Columbia University). 1965.

Yeh, Kung-chia. "Capital Formation." Economic Trends in Communist China. Edited by Eckstein, Galenson, and Liu. Chicago: Aldine, 1968.

MICHIGAN PAPERS IN CHINESE STUDIES

No. 1. The Chinese Economy, 1912-1949, by Albert Feuerwerker.

No. 2. The Cultural Revolution: 1967 in Review, four essays by Michel Oksenberg, Carl Riskin, Robert Scalapino, and Ezra Vogel.

No. 3. Two Studies in Chinese Literature: "One Aspect of Form in the Arias of Yüan Opera" by Dale Johnson; and "Hsü K'o's Huang Shan Travel Diaries" translated by Li Chi, with an introduction, commentary, notes, and bibliography by Chun-shu Chang.

No. 4. Early Communist China: Two Studies: "The Fu-t'ien Incident" by Ronald Suleski; and "Agararian Reform in Kwangtung, 1950-1953" by Daniel Bays.

No. 5. The Chinese Economy, ca. 1870-1911, by Albert Feuerwerker.

No. 6. Chinese Paintings in Chinese Publications, 1956-1968: An Annotated Bibliography and An Index to the Paintings, by E. J. Laing.

No. 7. The Treaty Ports and China's Modernization: What Went Wrong? by Rhoads Murphey.

No. 8. Two Twelfth Century Texts on Chinese Painting, "Shan-shui ch'un-ch'üan chi" by Han Cho, and chapters nine and ten of "Hua-chi" by Teng Ch'un, translated by Robert J. Maeda.

No. 9. The Economy of Communist China, 1949-1969, by Chu-yuan Cheng.

No. 10. Educated Youth and the Cultural Revolution in China by Martin Singer.

No. 11. Premodern China: A Bibliographical Introduction, by Chun-shu Chang.

No. 12. Two Studies on Ming History, by Charles O. Hucker.

No. 13. Nineteenth Century China: Five Imperialist Perspectives, selected by Dilip Basu, edited with an introduction by Rhoads Murphey.

No. 14. Modern China, 1840-1972: An Introduction to Sources and Research Aids, by Andrew J. Nathan.

No. 15. Women in China: Studies in Social Change and Feminism, edited with an introduction by Marilyn B. Young.

No. 16. An Annotated Bibliography of Chinese Painting Catalogues and Related Texts, by Hin-cheung Lovell.

No. 17. China's Allocation of Fixed Capital Investment, 1952-57, by Chu-yuan Cheng.

Price: $3.00 (US) each
except $3.50 for special issues #6 and #15

*   *   *

MICHIGAN ABSTRACTS OF CHINESE AND
JAPANESE WORKS ON CHINESE HISTORY

No. 1. The Ming Tribute Grain System by Hoshi Ayao, translated by Mark Elvin.

No. 2. Commerce and Society in Sung China by Shiba Yoshinobu translated by Mark Elvin.

No. 3. Transport in Transition: The Evolution of Traditional Shipping in China, translations by Andrew Watson.

No. 4. Japanese Perspectives on China's Early Modernization: The Self-Strengthening Movement, 1860-1895, by K. H. Kim.

Price: $3.50 (US) each

*   *   *

Michigan Papers and Abstracts available from:
Center for Chinese Studies
University of Michigan
Lane Hall
Ann Arbor, Michigan 48104
USA

DATE DUE

GAYLORD			PRINTED IN U.S.A.